READERS' COMMENTS

"*BOUNCING BACK!* is absolutely the most inspiring book I have ever read!"
       Jim Kalb, CEO, Triad Group, San Diego

"I've read hundreds of personal development books. All of them combined don't give me the inspiration, insight and peace of mind of Andrew Matthews' books. They saved my life. I have achieved more in one month than in forty years!"
       Peter Thompson, U. K.

"Reading your books was like a helping hand. One moment I was drowning, and then suddenly I felt safe. Thank you so very much!"
       Rosanna Monaco, Zurich, SWITZERLAND

"Your books changed my life when I was sixteen years old and going through depression. Now, I'll always be okay! Thanks so much!"
       Linda Lu, Valparaiso, CHILE

"I love *BOUNCING BACK!* It's like God-sent for recent times that I am struggling and almost giving up completely. It revived my faith!"
       Kristine Yeo, Malaysia

"Your books are helping me as a kind of miracle in all of my hard times. They have changed my life – and they have changed my friends' lives. I really love them!"
       Omid Mortazavi, IRAN

READERS' COMMENTS

"I read **BOUNCING BACK!** following a divorce. It was a complete lifesaver!"

Simon Jones, Tadley, UK

"Your books gave me a light when I was totally in darkness. They changed me and my view of life. Now, your books have become a kind of Bible for me... I want to express my REAL, DEEP APPRECIATION for your books and your message."

Moonsun Choi, KOREA

"Your books have already changed my life! They are so simple and straightforward that anyone can put them into practice immediately. I am now much happier and more self-confident."

Szymon Przedwojski, POLAND

"I devoured **BOUNCING BACK!** in one sitting! Inspiring, powerful. Truly a masterpiece. It reignited my dreams and visions."

Delphine Ang, Life Coach, SINGAPORE

"I was bed-ridden with terrible depression, my childhood was getting to me, my business was struggling. Then I read your books. It has completely changed my life. I now run a national consultancy business. I now appreciate each day. I am so grateful."

Adam Sanderson, Woore, U.K.

"I never thought self-help books were for me but, whoa, how wrong I was! I can't believe how my life has changed in all areas. I even landed my dream job with a major airline at 44!

Your books are easy, fun, enjoyable. I can apply these things EVERY DAY. Thank you, thank you!! You rock!"

Andy Jackson, Auckland, NEW ZEALAND

BOUNCING BACK!

written and illustrated by

Andrew Matthews

Seashell Publishers
Australia

Bouncing Back!
Copyright © 2024 by Andrew Matthews
and Seashell Publishers

Published by:
Seashell Publishers,
PO Box 325, Trinity Beach,
Queensland, Australia, 4879

Email: info@seashell.com.au
Visit Andrew's website: www.andrewmatthews.com

ISBN: 978-0-6458462-5-6

First printed Jan 2024
1st reprint March 2024
2nd reprint September 2024

No part of this publication, text or illustrations may be reproduced in any form or by any means, electronic, mechanical, photocopying, recording or otherwise, without the prior consent of the author and the publisher.

Andrew Matthews' other books include:
Being Happy!
Making Friends
Follow Your Heart
Happiness in a Nutshell
Being a Happy Teen
Happiness Now
Happiness in Hard Times
Stop the Bullying!
How Life Works

Printed in Malaysia by Vivar Printing

To You, My Readers:
Thank you for supporting me and reading my books these last 35 years. Thank you for all your letters and emails.
I am so grateful to you.

To Julie:
Julie, my wife and publisher – AGAIN, thank you!
Thank you for your wisdom, your courage and guidance. Thank you for the long hours you have worked and the sacrifices you have made to take our books to the world.

Thank You:
To Nicole MacSween, Jane Thomas, Jimmy Kalb, Joseph Engel, Dr George Blair-West, Penny Blair-West, Gloria Webb and Marie Martin, thank you for all your help with *BOUNCING BACK!*

CONTENTS

Chapter 1:
FIND PURPOSE 11
When Bad Luck Becomes Good Luck
How We Become Resilient
A Shocking Discovery

Chapter 2:
ACCEPT WHAT YOU CAN'T CHANGE 27
How Life Gets Better
Resentment
Accepting Ourselves
Needs and Wants

Chapter 3:
LOOK FOR GOOD THINGS EVERY DAY 53
Be Kind to Yourself
How Do Happy People Think?
How Do I Replace Negative Thoughts?

Chapter 4:
LIVE ONE DAY AT A TIME 77
How to Get Better at Anything
How Do I Find the Perfect Job?

Chapter 5:
EVERYBODY FAILS 97
Everybody Hurts
The BIG Lie
Let's Toughen Up!
What Other People Think

Chapter 6:
SET A TARGET 117
Why Set Goals?
It's What You Become
What Hurts Most?
Your Long-term Goal

Chapter 7:
IMAGINE A BETTER LIFE ... 139
Success Starts in Your Imagination
How We Create Life-changing Habits

Chapter 8:
WHAT NOW? 153

The 7 Steps to Bouncing Back:

1
Find Purpose in Whatever Happens
What makes us extraordinary?
Facing challenges we didn't choose.

2
Accept What You Can't Change
Acceptance allows us to move on.
Acceptance is power.

3
Look for Good Things Every Day
We find in life what we look for.

4
Live One Day at a Time
Don't worry about what you can't fix today.
Just give your best until bedtime.

5
When You Fall, Get Back up
Daily persistence creates surprising results.

6
Set a Target
It's not failure that crushes us.
What hurts most is never having tried.

7
Imagine a Better Life
For life to get better we must see it as better.
We become what we think about.

1

FIND PURPOSE IN WHATEVER HAPPENS

What makes us extraordinary?
Facing challenges we didn't choose.

How we become resilient.
What successful people have in common.

Julie

My wife, Julie, lost her mother at ten, following a long illness.

At eight-years-old, Julie was calling doctors, arranging ambulances, taking her mother to hospital. At eight-years-old, Julie was taking care of her brothers and sisters. She just learned to make things happen.

There's not a day that Julie doesn't think of her mother. Even today, when Julie talks of her mother, her voice cracks and tears roll down her face.

If my life ever depended on someone, I would want it to be Julie.

Julie once built an orphanage for 150 babies in Indonesia – *with no money.*

She visited construction companies and begged for materials. She would wait outside the offices of the owners and managers, sometimes all day. When they finally agreed to see her, she would tell them, *"I'm building an orphanage. I don't want your money. Give me whatever timber, bricks, window frames, doors or paint you can spare."*

The villagers gave their labour. Julie supervised the construction. Julie wasn't part of any international aid organisation. It was just Julie, all four-feet-eleven of her.

She would visit pharmaceutical companies and beg, "*I have a lot of sick children. Please give me whatever bandages, antiseptic, formula, drugs you can spare.*"

Sheets for the cots? She cut them from second-hand sheets, donated by local five-star hotels.

Julie built and stocked an entire orphanage without a cent.

Julie became my publisher in 1995. She said, "*Andrew, we're going global!*"

She knew nothing about publishing.

Thanks to Julie, my books are now in 48 languages.

What made her unstoppable?

She will say, "*Growing up without a mother. It was hard but it made me stronger.*"

Circumstances she didn't choose turned Julie into a force of nature.

*No one is **BORN** extraordinary. We **BECOME** extraordinary, resilient, unstoppable by conquering circumstances we didn't choose.*

It's a Disaster!

Eight-year-old Kieren was chasing his little brother around the house when he ran through a plate glass door. Kieren's left calf was shredded. Doctors feared he would lose the leg.

Eighty-seven stitches saved his leg, but Kieren couldn't walk or use crutches. Doctors told him to start swimming to strengthen the leg.

The little boy who hated putting his head in the water had no choice. He began swimming – and kept swimming. Kieren Perkins became one of the great distance swimmers of all time. He broke 11 world records and won two Olympic gold medals in the 1500 metres freestyle.

In a Nutshell

Most disasters are not TOTAL disasters.

Tiffany Was Robbed

One morning, Tiffany logged into her bank account and her own worst nightmare... her life savings were gone. She had been hacked.

Her bank said, *"There's nothing we can do!"* Tiffany was heartbroken, gutted.

Tiffany enrolled in cyber-security courses. She decided, *"I can save people from having my experience."* She started an online cyber-security newsletter for "dummies". She began with a mailing list of 12, which grew to hundreds.

Friends and neighbours would ask her advice, and soon strangers started seeking her help. Tiffany began charging for her time. Suddenly, she had a business!

Tiffany built a business website. Tiffany now consults with companies. She hosts their websites. Tiffany makes more in one month than she lost to the hackers.

Most disasters are not TOTAL disasters.

When Bad Luck Becomes Good Luck

Did you ever apply for a **job** – and not get it? And it turned out to be a good thing?

Did you ever have an **accident** – or land in hospital? And something good came from it?

Did you ever have your **travel plans** wrecked by bad weather or by an airline or by a pandemic? It seemed like a catastrophe, but it worked to your advantage.

Did you ever **get dumped** by a boyfriend who you thought was "Mr Right". You met him ten years later and realised, *"I dodged a bullet!"*

When We Have No Option

Here's how life works: we do what is convenient and we do things out of **habit**.

Then, disaster! Suddenly we are left with no job, or no money or no choice.

Finally, we:

- do what we were **too scared** to do
- do what we were **too lazy** to do
- do what we were **too comfortable** to do, or
- do what we **always wanted** to do.

In a Nutshell

So often, something seems like a setback – but good things can come from it.

Marco's Story

Marco worked in a furniture factory and hated it. His dream was to own a restaurant. But Marco never had the money or the courage to go out on his own.

Then Marco got sacked from the factory.

Jobless and broke, he sold his Toyota to pay the rent and pawned his guitar to feed his kids. When things got desperate, Marco moved his wife and two children into his parents' tiny apartment.

Says Marco, "*I felt useless. I couldn't even keep a job in a factory! I went into depression.*"

Marco took any work he could find: he washed cars, dishes and windows. Then he got a job in an Italian restaurant waiting on tables.

For the first time in his life, Marco loved going to work. The customers loved Marco, and Marco loved them. Marco found confidence he never knew he had. Within a year, Marco was manager.

And today? Marco's boss made him a partner in the restaurant. Marco is living his dream and serving the best spaghetti marinara in town.

Debbie's Story... and a Question

Debbie was a bright and happy teen, an A student. Her classmates voted her *the student most likely to succeed.*

At sixteen, Debbie announced to her parents, *"I'm pregnant."*

Mum was devastated. Dad was furious. The whole family said, *"What a disaster!"*

Debbie quit school to raise her baby, Jack. Mum said, *"You had such a bright future. What a disaster!"*

At seventeen, Debbie married the baby's father. Everyone agreed, *"It's a disaster."*

The young couple was miserable and soon divorced. Everyone said, *"We told you it was a disaster!"*

Debbie recalls, *"I felt I had let myself and my family down. I felt alone and ashamed."*

At 23, Debbie decided her mission was to help teenage mothers. She finished high school, and then got a degree in psychology. She now works with an agency that supports and inspires teenage unmarried mothers. Says Debbie, *"I know what these girls are going through, and I can help. I feel like I was born to do this."*

Debbie now has a devoted partner, a meaningful job and a loving relationship with her parents.

Debbie's son, Jack, is the light of her life and her parents' pride and joy.

Quick Quiz: *Which bit was the disaster for Debbie?* **Was it:**

- Having baby, Jack, who became the joy of her life?
- Postponing her education to study something that she really cared about?
- The collapse of her first marriage that taught her what matters in a relationship?

Debbie would say, *"Things that SEEMED LIKE disasters helped shape the good life I have now."*

Jessie's Story

Jessie was 19, and on vacation in Hawaii with friends. They were hiking through the jungle and came across a waterfall. Someone said, *"Let's jump in!"* Says Jessie:

> It seemed like a fun thing to do! When I hit the water, one of my vertebrae exploded into 14 pieces. My life exploded into pieces, too.
>
> I was immobilised for two weeks. I needed surgery to remove the bone fragments and two disks, and then fuse three vertebrae together and drill six three-inch metal rods into my spine. The risks of the eight-hour procedure were lung perforation, paralysis and death. But it wasn't like I had a choice. As the anaesthetist put me under, I wondered if she would be the last person I saw. When I awoke after surgery, I was filled with deep, profound gratitude – and then a lot of pain! The new hardware was like an iron fist, squeezing my spine. I couldn't sleep because everything hurt, and I couldn't eat because the medication made me nauseous. I lost 11 kilograms in two weeks.
>
> My body healed in months, but then my mind and soul were the ones that needed rehabilitation. From the outside I seemed well again. But I felt disconnected from reality. Something was wrong, but I didn't know what. Unfortunately, no one else did, either.
>
> It led me on a path to try to understand how my body works. I wanted to know what I could do to wake up in the morning feeling amazing."[1]

Jessie studied biochemistry in Paris and then worked for five years in a genetics laboratory in California. She learned a lot about how our bodies work. She discovered that glucose levels in the body are critical for everyone, not just for diabetics. What Jessie learned in the laboratory, she used to help heal herself from the inside out.

She gathered her research into a book. In 2022, Jessie Inchauspé's, *Glucose Revolution*, became an international bestseller.

Bouncing Back

Sometimes disasters give us a lifelong purpose.

The King and the Boulder

Zen Buddhists tell of an ancient king who grew unhappy with the citizens of his kingdom. His people had become lazy and soft, and he decided to teach them a lesson.

The king organised for a big boulder to be placed across the only road into the city. He then hid nearby to see how the townsfolk would react.

A crowd soon gathered at the boulder, and several people made weak attempts to shift the big rock. Others simply complained: *"What bad luck!" "The king should fix the roads!"*

Eventually, a poor peasant came by. He pushed and shoved the boulder with all his might – but it wouldn't budge. The peasant disappeared into a nearby forest and returned with a log.

He placed the log against the big rock and pulled it, like a big lever. He struggled and strained – and behold! The boulder rolled aside.

Beneath the boulder the peasant found a gift from the king – a purse filled with gold – and a note:

> *"The obstacle in the path becomes the path. Never forget: within every obstacle is the opportunity to improve our situation."*

How We Become Resilient

Why do some people give up and others keep going?

A guy breaks his finger and moans, *"This is terrible!"* His wife breaks her back and says, *"This is just a hiccup!"*

Think of people you admire:

- people who have achieved big things
- people who always bounce back, or
- people who are unusually kind.

You'll notice something. They weren't BORN extraordinary. They BECAME extraordinary through difficult circumstances.

Maybe they:

- lost parents early in life
- grew up in poverty
- went broke
- lost their home
- lost their business, or
- survived serious illness.

They were shaped by circumstances they didn't choose!

My Dad

My father lost his mother when he was seven, and he was sent to live with a foster family.

I imagine him, a sad little boy, aching for his mother, missing his three brothers and wondering, "*Why doesn't my Daddy want me?*"

At 19 Dad joined the navy – and then the Second World War broke out. He was sent to war.

Dad spent five years having bombs dropped on him. Ships went down around him. His mates died around him. Dad never knew which day would be his last.

On one ship, they had nothing to eat for two weeks but porridge!

Dad returned from the war a changed man, shocked by what he had seen and grateful to be alive. He would tell me, "*People worry too much about little things that don't matter.*"

Dad would say, "*As long as I've got a dry bed to sleep in, I'm happy!*"

I used to wonder, "*Why does Dad never stress about little things? How did he become so resilient?*"

Because of his childhood and the war – circumstances he didn't choose.

The Questions We Ask

You say, "*How do I bounce back from failure, tragedy, disappointment?*" It has a lot to do with the questions you ask. Some people wonder, "*Why do bad things always happen to me?*" That question doesn't help.

Better questions are:
- "*What am I learning?*"
- "*How will this make me stronger?*"

Character

Did you ever look in the mirror and say, "*I wish I had a different face... body... nose!*"?

Did you ever ask yourself, *"How come other people are so talented and brilliant? How come I don't feel good about myself?"*

Many of us have these thoughts!

But here's the crunch: talent and beauty are useful. But there are plenty of talented and beautiful people whom we don't admire – and who are of little help in a crisis.

The qualities most of us value above all others are HONESTY, COURAGE, PERSISTENCE, GENEROSITY, HUMILITY, RESILIENCE and KINDNESS.

You'll notice something about this entire list. We aren't BORN with these qualities. We DEVELOP them. Often, we are taught them.

Do you want more self-respect? You simply work at developing your own honesty, determination, generosity, humility, courage, resilience and kindness. It is called "character".

How do we develop character? By dealing with setbacks and disappointments.

Anyone can be nice when they just got promoted. Anyone can be nice when they just won a lottery. Character is revealed in bad times.

At 25 I made a shocking discovery... the HAPPIEST people I knew had BIGGER PROBLEMS than me.

Can you be gracious when things aren't going well? Can you be kind when other people aren't? Can you be nice in a traffic jam?

Can you get your mind off your own problems long enough to be a good friend?

A Shocking Discovery

I grew up believing that when I had fewer problems, I would be happier. Then, at 25 I made a shocking discovery: the happiest people I knew had bigger problems than me!

Have you noticed the same thing?

The people who find the most joy and the most meaning in life have usually suffered tragedy, gone broke, bounced back from cancer, or lost loved ones way too soon.

This proves that it's not **WHAT HAPPENS** to you that matters. It's **HOW YOU THINK ABOUT what happens** to you.

Bouncing Back

What you thought was BREAKING you is probably MAKING you!

OTHER PEOPLE'S LIVES **MAY LOOK PERFECT** FROM A DISTANCE.

DON'T BE FOOLED.

WE ALL HAVE OUR FAMILY CRISES, STRUGGLES AND HEARTACHES.

"If Only My Life Was Easier!"

Last week, Adam came to our home to install some sliding doors.

Adam was a professional motorbike racer for 20 years, and he recently sold a successful business. He owns real estate.

I said to him, *"You don't NEED to work! Why are you working for this company installing sliding doors?"*

He smiled. He said, *"I retired! Suddenly I began to worry about stupid little things that don't matter. I couldn't sleep."*

He said, *"I needed **purpose**. I needed **connection to people**. I needed **satisfaction at the end of every day**."*

He said, *"I happened to meet the boss of this door company."* I asked him, *"Can I try working for you? I'll work for nothing for a month."* Adam said, *"I have been here five months. I am so much happier!"*

He said, "WHEN YOU DON'T HAVE A PURPOSE, YOU WORRY ABOUT STUFF THAT DOESN'T MATTER."

The Fantasy

We may imagine that the perfect life means floating around on a cruise ship with no responsibilities.

It sounds good. But spend a few months on the cruise ship, and you too may begin to stress about details that don't matter, such as, *"Why is room service ten minutes late?"*

In a Nutshell

We all need purpose, connection and a feeling of contribution.

"But the World Is Going Crazy! How Can I Be Happy?"

When would you rather be alive?

Would you rather be living through the Great Depression with worldwide unemployment? It lasted nearly ten years.

Or would you prefer the Second World War that raged for six years? Eighty million people died.

If you were born in 1800, your life expectancy was 38 years. At 19, you were middle-aged! Would you want that?

We have our challenges. Now is still a good time to be alive.

Life Happens in Waves

Are you struggling right now? Maybe your relationship broke up. Maybe your refrigerator blew up, and your car broke down, and you hate your job, and you just want to quit.

Here's the good news: things will get better because life happens in waves. Bills and wedding invitations come in waves. New opportunities come in waves. Grief comes in waves. Everything comes in waves – even waves come in waves.

2

ACCEPT WHAT YOU CAN'T CHANGE

Acceptance allows us to move on.
Acceptance is power.

What keeps us stuck?
How do happy people think?

Michael's Story

My wife, Julie, has a son, Michael. My stepson.

At 18 Michael was fit, handsome, ambitious. He was driving down a highway one afternoon when his car hit a truck. The impact tore the roof off Michael's car. He was rushed by ambulance to the Royal Adelaide Hospital with head injuries. At 6.00 pm, four surgeons called a meeting. The doctors told Julie, *"Your son is brain-dead."*

What does "brain-dead" mean to a mother?

They said, *"He won't live past midnight."* They said, *"We want your permission to take his organs. He can help a lot of people."*

When four doctors say, *"We want his organs,"* what does a mother do?

Julie told the doctors, *"My job is to save my son. You cannot take his organs. You must be able to do something!"*

The surgeons said, *"His brain is swelling inside his skull. It's killing him!"*

Julie insisted, *"You must be able to do something! Can you remove a piece of his skull to relieve the pressure?"*

Reluctantly, the surgeons operated and removed a part of Michael's skull.

At 11.00 pm Michael's lungs collapsed. The doctors called another meeting. They said, "*Both his lungs have collapsed, as we feared they would. He is brain-dead. He is on a respirator.*"

They said, "*We would like to take his organs.*"

This time they had a form for Julie to sign. Julie begged them, "*Keep him alive for three days, and you will never see me again.*"

That was Monday. The following Thursday at midday we gathered at the hospital to say goodbye. We had a priest to give Michael his last rites. They switched off the respirator.

Michael breathed!

Michael survived – severely disabled. He was totally paralysed on his right side. He had half of his sight. He couldn't speak. He had to learn to walk all over again.

He struggled, we struggled. We spent 25 years helping him to speak. He still has trouble saying a full sentence. He still struggles to remember things. Michael will never have a regular job.

Focus on What You Have

Boys that Michael went to school with are lawyers and bankers and tennis coaches. Julie had similar dreams for Michael.

People say to Julie, "*How do you deal with it? How do you deal with having a severely disabled son?*" Julie says, "I STILL HAVE HIM."

Julie's reply is always, *"He is a beautiful soul, he is a loving son, he is kind, he's generous."*

How does Julie survive with a severely disabled son?

SHE FOCUSES ON WHAT SHE HAS.

What is the alternative? Be angry? Be bitter?
Focus on what you have. Is it logical? No.
Is it realistic? Probably not.

Michael imagined a different life for himself. Today, Michael has one good leg and one good arm. He has half his sight and half his hearing. He can't speak like you or me.

Michael goes to the gym five days a week, he has speech lessons each Wednesday, he catches the bus, he shops, he cooks, he cleans, he walks three kilometres every day. Michael keeps doing the best he can.

In a Nutshell

We accept what we can't change, and we change what we can.

How Life Gets Better

Maybe you are broke right now.
Maybe you have lost your job. Maybe you worry about the future.

Have You Lost Someone?

Perhaps you have lost family or friends, and you are grieving. Maybe you wonder, *"Will my life ever be the same?"*

When we lose a loved one, we may go through several stages of grieving, including denial, anger and depression.

Dealing with Any Loss

We don't just grieve when we lose loved ones. We grieve when we lose anything precious. If you have lost your job or a beautiful relationship, or if you have lost your good health, it hurts. You may be going through many things:

Denial: *"This can't be happening." "This is too terrible!"*

Anger: *"Why me?" "It's not fair!"*

Depression: *"I feel so sad." "There's no hope!"*

Bargaining with God or Your Surgeon: *"Please bring her back..." "Promise me I'll survive..."*

If illness or tragedy has turned your world upside down, it hurts! If you are feeling lost, angry, depressed, you are NORMAL!

This book is about bouncing back from everyday disasters and disappointments. If you have been hit by a once-in-a-lifetime tragedy, this book may help, but it will never be enough. You need a lot of love, support and, perhaps, professional help.

Why professional help? Because counsellors can see things that our friends and family can't. Professionals can say things that friends and family can't say – or won't say. That's why counsellors, psychologists and psychiatrists can often help us move on.

Pain and Grieving

Here's what experts have shared with me: we grieve for WHAT COULD HAVE BEEN.

For example:

- We lose a loved one and grieve over a beautiful life cut short – or we grieve for a future we planned but will never see.
- We lose a job and grieve: *"I could have had a great career."*
- We lose our good health and grieve: *"I will never run again."*
- We end a relationship and grieve: *"We could have been so happy together."*

Grieving is not the same as sadness. SADNESS is an *EMOTION*. GRIEVING is a *HEALING PROCESS*.

Does everyone need to talk about their loss?

Not everybody wants to talk about their loss. But we all need to grieve somehow.

What happens if we don't grieve?

Take a soldier who loses his buddies in battle and takes no time to grieve. He pretends he is fine, but he carries a lot of sadness, fear, anger, guilt. He is irritable and he lashes out at people he loves. Anything can trigger his temper – especially any talk of the war. He dulls the pain with drugs and/or alcohol.

When we don't take time to grieve, we suffer, much like the soldier. We stay stuck, much like the soldier.

You can lock down your emotions and "tough it out". But when you shut down sadness, you shut down happiness.

You will never flourish in a new relationship if you never resolve the loss of your last one. You will never thrive in a new job if you never accept the loss of your last one.

Why does crying help?

People think crying is weak. They could not be more wrong. It takes strength to unlock big emotions.

Crying cleanses us. It is healing. It is a gift.

When my sister, Jane, was diagnosed with breast cancer she saw a counsellor. Jane told me:

> "He was helpful and encouraging. He shook my hand at the end of the first appointment and said, 'Congratulations! You've been crying for three-quarters of an hour and haven't apologised once.' We both laughed. I didn't feel so bad after that."

How Do I Grieve for Lost Loved Ones?

People feel the pain in their own time. People grieve differently.

Some people visit a grave site with flowers and pour their hearts out. Some people create a little shrine in their home where they will sit with a photo of their loved one. Some listen to their loved one's favourite music and let the tears flow. Some people light a candle every evening and sit with a glass of wine and remember. Some people grieve by cooking their loved one's favourite pasta.

Some people gather every year, on an anniversary, with family and friends who understand.

ACCEPTANCE

Here's the critical part of the grieving process: **ACCEPTANCE**.

Acceptance doesn't mean, "*I like what happened.*"
Acceptance doesn't always mean, "*I like where I am.*"
Acceptance means, "*I realise my life may never be the same.*"
Acceptance means, "*This is where I am – and now I move on.*"

You say, "*I just don't know what to do!*"

Here is the first thing to do: you accept where you are. For things to get better, you first make peace with your situation.

Forget about blame, forget about guilt, forget the "*What ifs?*"

Acceptance isn't *giving up*.

Acceptance is recognition that, "*This is a part of my journey*". Very often it means, "*Right now I have no idea why this had to be a part of my journey, but I embrace it anyway.*"

Sometimes you just want to quit. That's when you either:

- Give up, or
- Change how you think, and change what you are doing.

Bouncing Back

You can only change what you acknowledge. This means ACCEPTANCE is POWER.

"It Should Be Different!"

Unhappy people like to argue with reality. They say things like:

- *"It shouldn't have happened."*
- *"People should appreciate me."*
- *"The government should fix it."*

That doesn't help.

FLEXIBILIY

HAPPY PEOPLE DON'T EXPECT EVERYONE TO AGREE WITH THEM.

THEY DON'T DEMAND THAT LIFE BE PERFECTLY PREDICTABLE.

THEY ARE HAPPY WHEN IT'S SUNNY. THEY ARE HAPPY WHEN IT'S RAINING.

IT'S CALLED "ACCEPTING WHAT YOU CAN'T CHANGE".

Thomas Edison

"*Go get your mother and all her friends. They'll never see a fire like this again.*"

Thomas Edison invented the original record player and the motion picture camera. He also developed the electric light bulb and a thousand other inventions or patents. Thomas even built the world's first movie production studio.

Edison's parents were poor, he had no education, and by the age of 12 he was almost totally deaf. It seems he also had ADHD. At 19, Edison was fired from Western Union for spilling acid on the office floor.

Thomas Edison had a bad start and every reason to fail.

Instead, he founded 14 companies, including General Electric, and built a business empire. Edison's inventions changed the world. What made him unusual?

For one thing, he knew how to bounce back.

On December 10, 1914, there was an explosion at Edison's massive factory/laboratory in West Orange, New Jersey. Ten buildings caught fire. Eight fire departments battled flames six and seven stories high.

Fuelled by the chemicals onsite, the firestorm destroyed "fireproof" concrete buildings. Edison and his son, Charles, arrived to see the blaze incinerating records, prototypes, machinery, stock, furniture.

In today's money, the damage was about 30 million dollars' worth.

As green and yellow flames leapt skyward, Edison turned to his son with almost childlike excitement: "*Go get your mother and all her friends. They'll never see a fire like this again!*"

Edison understood, "*We can't change this. Let's enjoy the fire!*" That's instant acceptance.

Later that night, Edison told the New York Times, "*Although I am over 67 years old, I'll start all over again tomorrow.*"

Edison was back at work next morning. Within three weeks, part of his plant was operational. Employees worked double shifts. The plant was soon producing more than ever.

In a Nutshell

What is it that you DON'T LIKE AND CAN'T CHANGE? How long do you want to wait before you accept it?

Steve Bounces Back

My friend, Steve, had a plan: retire from teaching and play the over 50s tennis circuit around Southeast Asia.

But Steve had worn out the cartilage in both knees – it was bone on bone. He had chronic arthritis.

Steve had double surgery and got two brand-new titanium knees.

Says Steve, "*The pain was horrendous. For the first six months, I barely slept. For 18 months, I could hardly walk.*

"*Metal knees feel very heavy. Three years after surgery, I couldn't jump even one inch off the ground. I had always been an athlete. Now I was crippled! I was shattered and depressed.*

"*No one could advise me if – or how – a guy with two metal knees could return to tournament tennis.*"

Whatever it Takes

Steve put a gym in his house and designed an exercise routine to strengthen his legs. He worked out for hours every day. He got back on the court.

Steve can now jump over your coffee table. Last month he won a big tournament in Japan. His current world ranking is 29.

Says Steve, "*My dad had polio as a child and didn't walk until he was 15. His mum wrote to doctors in America for a treatment program which they followed every day. My dad – the kid that couldn't walk – became a tennis champion. Dad is my inspiration.*"

Steve is now creating videos to help other athletes bounce back from total knee replacements.

ACCEPTANCE can mean: "*I would never choose this, but I am going to beat it, and then I WILL HELP OTHERS BEAT IT.*"

What helps ease the pain? Helping other people.

"RESENTMENT IS LIKE DRINKING POISON AND WAITING FOR THE OTHER PERSON TO DIE."

St. Augustine

Resentment

Were you ever told that it's a good idea to forgive people? You might have even been told that it is a holy or spiritual thing to do.

But there is a more basic reason to forgive people: when you *don't* forgive them, it ruins *your* life!

Take Mary. Mary's boss gives her the sack. She vows, "*I'll never forgive the bastard!*" Who suffers? Not him!

Take Dave. Dave's girl runs off with his buddy. Dave swears, "*I'll never forgive her!*" Who suffers? Not her. Dave is losing sleep. She's at the movies!

Where do we get the idea that if WE don't forgive people, THEY suffer?

Is forgiving people easy? Usually not. But you don't forgive people for their benefit. You do it for your benefit.

YOU DON'T FORGIVE PEOPLE BECAUSE THEY **APOLOGISED** OR BECAUSE YOU **AGREE** WITH WHAT THEY DID OR BECAUSE IT'S **"SPIRITUAL"**.

YOU FORGIVE SO **YOU** CAN **MOVE ON**.

AND IT CAN BE HARD.

The events that transform us are never the things we would choose.

There is another reason why forgiveness is hard. Forgiving other people is usually about forgiving ourselves too. If I am angry with you, some part of me is angry with myself because I didn't do better.

This makes it doubly important that we choose to forgive.

Bouncing Back

To forgive someone, you don't have to agree with what they did. You just have to want your life to work.

Nelson Mandela

"I knew if I didn't leave my bitterness and hatred behind, I would still be in prison."

South African activist, Nelson Mandela, had every reason to be resentful.

Mandela began fighting for racial equality in the 1950s. When his organisation, the African National Congress, was outlawed in 1962, he was thrown in jail on Robben Island.

Mandela did 17 years of hard labour in a lime quarry. "Hard labour" is another word for, *"We will break you!"* For example, Mandela was made to dig huge holes under the burning sun, and then told to fill them in.

After 22 years in prison, the government said, *"Mr Mandela, if you stop campaigning for racial equality, you can go free."*

Mandela said, *"No, thank you!"* He stayed in jail for another five years, until the African National Congress was made legal, and he was released.

When Mandela became President of South Africa in 1994, people wondered, *"What revenge will he take against the violent apartheid regime that imprisoned him for 27 years?"*

Mandela chose forgiveness. He even invited his jailer, Paul Gregory, to his inauguration.

In 1993 Mandela was awarded the Nobel Peace Prize.

Leila Abdallah

Leila Abdallah was a mother of six. In February 2020 her children went for a walk to buy ice creams.

They were walking on the footpath when an out-of-control vehicle driven by a drunken driver left the road and hit the children.

Three of Leila's children – Antony, Angelina and Siena – died, as well as their little cousin, Veronique.

A year after the tragedy, Leila was interviewed on national television. She said:

> "We still have other kids depending on us – Liana, Alex and Michael... I am still blessed... the last year has been very hard.
>
> Since day one I have forgiven the driver and I don't hate him. I always pray for the driver because, to be honest with you, forgiveness is a sign of strength.
>
> And because I forgave him, I was able to focus on my kids rather than focusing on him. And forgiving him has allowed me to focus on them and has given me this sense of strength to keep going for the rest of my kids.
>
> We want to bring this positive energy to our kids because any decision [my husband] Danny and I take at the moment can impact generations – for not only our kids but also our grandkids, and we want to give them a positive life.
>
> It's not fair on them to be robbed of their joy, robbed of the happiness from their lives.
>
> There's a strength in forgiveness, there's a power in forgiveness.
>
> We are all hurting, and we are all suffering. Everyone suffers in a different way.
>
> Why spend the rest of your life in anger with a grudge? Why not let go and live in peace?
>
> Life is too short. We are all human, and we all do mistakes in life, and we all deserve forgiveness, and we all deserve another chance.
>
> Why am I going to hold a grudge over something I have no control over?
>
> I may as well be a strong person and move forward in my life for the rest of my family."[2]

We may say, *"If I was Leila, I would never forgive that driver!"*

But Leila's reasoning makes perfect sense. Maybe Leila can inspire us to forgive people for smaller things.

Greg's Story

As a child I felt let-down, shattered and scared. My mum was an alcoholic, and my dad had no interest in anything.

My brothers, Jim and Don, were much older than I was. They were great sportsmen and had lots of girlfriends. They were my heroes. I was so proud to be their little brother.

Then they both got into drugs. They became heroin addicts and drug traffickers. Dealers would come to our home demanding money. Jim and Don were in and out of jail for burglary and trafficking. I was ashamed whenever they made the TV news. I was ashamed that I spent my childhood visiting jails.

My dad only ever criticised us. When he came to watch me play football, he criticised everything I did. He told us, "*Education is useless!*"

From Bad to Worse

My parents split up when I was 13, and I went to live with my mum in a caravan. Mum had given up. Mum would stay in bed for weeks at a time. She told me, *"You are old enough to look after yourself."* I did my best to take care of her.

I did what I could to help Dad who by now had a brain tumour. Ultimately, Don was murdered, and Jim died from drug abuse.

My One Chance

My family was the perfect example of "how not to live". So I created my own life. I studied, I worked part-time. The day I graduated with a degree in chemistry, I was so proud! My feet barely touched the ground.

At 35, I had a family and a career, but I was crippled with resentment. I resented my dad for his disinterest. I was angry and ashamed of my brothers for being criminals, for ruining their lives and embarrassing me.

I was stuck. It seemed there was just one thing I could do to free myself. I had to forgive my dad and my brothers. I decided to hold a memorial ceremony in their honour.

My wife and daughters, my parents-in-law and I went to their gravesites, and I spoke about all the good things they had each achieved. I told my family how much I loved my dad and my brothers – and why I loved them.

It was a huge relief to let go of all that anger! It was like an exorcism.

I cried like I had never cried before. A massive weight lifted from my shoulders and my heart. I felt cleansed and much, much happier.

How important was it to forgive my family?

It's probably the reason that I am still alive today.

Kathleen's Story

Have you ever felt like a victim? Spare a thought for Kathleen.

She married Craig Folbigg in 1987, and they had four children.

Their first boy, Caleb, died at 19 days old. Their second, Patrick died at eight months. Their third child, Sarah, died at ten months. Their youngest, Laura, died at 18 months.

In 2001, Kathleen Folbigg was arrested for murder. Her trial was in 2003.

Although there was no evidence that Kathleen had ever hurt her babies, she was found guilty of murder and sentenced to forty years' jail for smothering each of her children.

Kathleen was suddenly *"Australia's worst female serial killer"*.

But every year, more experts began to question Kathleen's conviction.

She remained behind bars. In 2021 Kathleen was savagely beaten by another inmate.

New Evidence

Finally, in 2021, a petition, signed by one hundred leading scientists, was published by the Australian Academy of Sciences. The petition provided compelling explanations for each of the babies' deaths.

A 2021 enquiry into her trial considered fresh evidence based on recent scientific advances. It concluded:

- Kathleen's two girls both carried the "CALM2" genetic mutation that altered their heart rhythm. This, in combination with respiratory illnesses, likely led to their sudden and unexpected deaths.
- Kathleen's two boys carried the BSN gene which can cause early onset of epilepsy and death.

On June 6, 2023, Kathleen was given an unconditional pardon and released from jail.

Kathleen spent 20 years in jail for crimes she didn't commit. She grieved alone for her lost babies. Meanwhile, she was branded a monster.

Was Kathleen resentful and bitter?

In a video statement she said: *"I am extremely humbled and extremely grateful for being pardoned and released from prison... my eternal gratitude goes to my friends and family... I would not have survived this whole ordeal without them...*

"Today is a victory for science, and especially truth.

"I have forever and will always think of my children, grieve for my children, and have missed them and loved them terribly."

Bouncing Back

Says Kathleen, "I'd like people to take away a message that you can survive it, you can move on from it. The future is everything."

Forgiveness

Maybe forgiveness seems like a good idea for OTHER PEOPLE.

Do you feel resentful or angry over something or somebody?

Maybe a partner let you down, or maybe you missed out on a promotion, or maybe you feel that someone cheated you – or maybe you feel that life has cheated you.

What are the consequences of not accepting what has already happened? What has it cost to you – in lost opportunities, sleepless nights and lost happiness?

Is it time to forgive and move on?

DO I NEED TO LOVE MYSELF?

*YOU NEED TO AT LEAST **LIKE** YOURSELF!*

*WHY? BECAUSE WE **CREATE** THE LIFE WE **FEEL WE DESERVE**.*

Accepting Ourselves

Have you noticed what happens on days when you are angry with yourself? That's when you stub your toe on the doorstep and lose your house keys. That's when people abuse you on the train. When you give yourself a hard time, people give you a hard time.

When we concentrate on our own faults, the world keeps punishing us, and we keep punishing ourselves. We do it with ill health, with poverty, with loneliness.

When we don't like ourselves, the world doesn't like us. And then we blame the world.

It All Starts with You

It's not about your relationship with others. It's more about your relationship with you.

You say, *"Do I need to LOVE myself?"*

You need to at least LIKE yourself.

Why? Because we create the life we feel we deserve.

Quit seeing yourself as guilty.

Loving yourself means forgiving yourself for not getting everything right. It means admitting, *"To this point I have lived my life the best way I knew how."*

Bouncing Back

Forget perfection and aim for improvement.

Nick Vujicic

Nick Vujicic was born with no arms and no legs. Says Nick, *"For the longest, loneliest time, I wondered if there was anyone on earth like me, and whether there was any purpose to my life other than pain and humiliation."*

Nick wondered, *"Who would employ me? How will I ever find a wife?"* Relentlessly bullied at school, he attempted suicide.

Then, when still in his teens, he began to change his focus. Instead of focusing on what he couldn't do, he asked himself, *"Why not focus on what I CAN do?"* What he could do was help people put their own problems in perspective.

Nick wrote to over seventy schools, offering to give a motivational speech to the students. Seventy schools said, *"NO!"*

Nick persisted. He began telling his story to church groups and small student groups. These days he fills convention centres worldwide.

Nick has written international best-selling books including *Life Without Limits*. He created a worldwide charity for people with physical disabilities, called *Life Without Limbs*.

In 2012, Nick married Kanae. They have four children.

In a Nutshell

Forget about what you CAN'T do! Focus on what you CAN do.

Beauty in Imperfection

"The world breaks everyone, and afterward, many are strong at the broken places."

Ernest Hemingway

According to legend, around 1400 AD, the Japanese shogun, Ashikaga Yoshimitsu, broke his favourite tea bowl and sent it to China for repair.

When the bowl was returned, he was unhappy to see that ugly metal staples had been used to join the broken pieces. Shogun Yoshimitsu asked his own craftsmen to find a better way to fix his bowl. His artisans glued the pieces together with tree resin and gold leaf – and so the art of Kintsugi was born.

In Kintsugi, the faults are a feature. You don't try to hide the damage or pretend the accident never happened.

Kintsugi is not simply a way to repair pottery. It is...

A Way of Seeing

Kintsugi is rooted in the Zen philosophy of Wabi Sabi.

In Wabi Sabi we accept and respect what is damaged, scarred, vulnerable or old.

Cheryl Hunter suggests it's a way of embracing our imperfections.

Cheryl's Story

Cheryl grew up on a remote horse ranch in Colorado. She longed for the excitement of the city. She dreamed of being a model. Cheryl and her friend, Lizzie, saved their money and headed for Europe. She says:

> No sooner had we arrived in France than a man wearing a camera around his neck approached me. He asked me if I was a model. He told me he could make me one if I would just go off with him and his friend. I thought, "That's how

easy it is to become a model in France!"

Lizzy said, *"No way in hell!"* So I ditched her, and went off with the guy and his camera and his friend.

They drugged me. They took me to an abandoned construction site, and they beat me mercilessly. They drugged me again and raped me repeatedly. And they cut me.

They dumped me in a park in Nice three days later.

I didn't tell anybody; I couldn't tell anybody. I was now disgusting and dirty and filthy and ruined and used up – and if anybody knew what had happened to me, that's how they would see me.

I told no one. I just pushed it all down.

Cheryl eventually became a model. She lived and worked in seven countries. Her photos adorned glamour magazines. She was the worldwide Coca-Cola girl. She recalls:

I became very, very aloof and removed. I was a loner. Being a model suited me. Never once in all the years that I was a model did anyone ask me to have a deep conversation.

A Life-changing Conversation

One day while modelling in Japan, Cheryl was sitting in a conference room, admiring a big old wooden table. It had massive dents and nicks and divets, and it was narrow at one end.

An elderly couple took the time to share some Japanese wisdom that for Cheryl would be life-changing. She recalls:

They explained to me the concept of Wabi Sabi: *"The beauty of any object lies in the flaws of that object – mistakes or damages or ruined parts. The beauty is in the contrasts. So something is only perfect because it is balanced by imperfection."*

I wondered, '*Does this mean Wabi Sabi could even apply to me?*'[3]

Today, Cheryl Hunter owns and operates a media agency. She is a writer, TV producer and popular conference presenter.

What key thought helped Cheryl heal? And what is her message for us?

"You are magnificent, and what makes you magnificent is everything you previously believed is wrong with you."

Accepting Others

As you begin to forgive yourself for not being perfect, so you begin to accept others for not being perfect.

How do you love someone? Try substituting the word, "acceptance".

Total acceptance is unconditional love.

"I DON'T WANT YOU TO FIX ME. I WANT YOU TO LOVE THE BROKEN PIECES."

Jeff Hood

Jim

When I met Jim, he had a BIG business, a BIG house and a BIG art collection. He and his wife threw BIG parties and took BIG vacations.

Jim sold his BIG business to a BIG company that didn't pay him the final BIG instalment. Jim spent half his fortune on a BIG legal case – and the other half on a BIG divorce.

Jim now lives in a small apartment with a small dog.

We met in the supermarket the other day. He told me, "*I am happier today than I have ever been. I have learnt three things:*

- *"I don't have to impress anybody."*
- *"My life is different today than it was – and that is okay."*
- *"There is a time for everything."*

Needs and Wants

It's normal to WANT things. It is healthy to WANT a better life. WANTS are what DRIVE us. Setting goals is part of what makes us human.

But there is a difference between WANTS and NEEDS.

Here are things you may NEED:

- a roof over your head
- two or three meals a day
- clothes and shoes
- a safe, reliable car
- a job
- education and medical care for your family
- money for essentials.

Here are things you may WANT:

- a bigger home
- an expensive car
- the latest smart phone
- overseas vacations.

What can make us unhappy? Focusing on stuff that OTHER PEOPLE HAVE that we don't.

Many of us grow up with a mental program: *If you're not happy, GET SOMETHING, BUY SOMETHING* – *buy a better car, get a bigger boat.*

Often, the solution is not about getting more, but about focusing on what we have.

There are two ways of managing our WANTS:

> Option A. "*I WANT that – and I* won't be happy *until I get it!*"
>
> Option B. "*I WOULD LIKE THAT – and I* will be happy *whether I get it or not.*"

Option B works better. The challenge of life is to be happy with what you have while you pursue what you want.

In a Nutshell

Getting more stuff rarely leads to peace of mind. Mostly, GETTING MORE STUFF *leads to* WANTING MORE STUFF.

> To have a beautiful life you
> don't need lots of stuff.
> It's more about embracing the
> moment, seeing the best in people
> and believing life will turn out well.

Nature Heals

People try lots of things to help them feel better – including drugs, alcohol, gambling and too much pizza – and they don't help.

Almost no one ever went for a walk in a park or on a beach, and came back and said, "*I feel worse.*"

*When life hurts, nature heals.
Ocean breezes and peaceful
forests restore us.
Walk on the beach or sit in a park.
You'll think better thoughts.
There is nothing to figure out.
It just happens.*

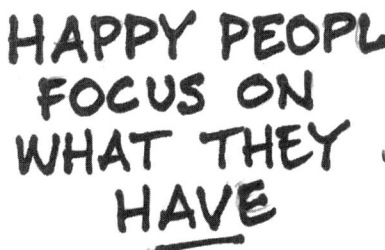

3

LOOK FOR GOOD THINGS EVERY DAY

We find in life what we look for.

Why "events" don't make us happy.
Does gratitude help?

Rob

The taxi driver greeted me with a big smile.

"I'm Rob."

He was so cheerful! I asked him, *"Did you always have this happy attitude?"*

He said, *"I was the WORST. I was a moody, miserable pain in the arse."*

I asked, *"What happened?"*

He said, *"I have an 11-year-old son, Johnny."*

When Johnny was five, Johnny told my ex-wife, *"I don't want to see Daddy anymore."* My ex-wife said, *"Why not?"* Johnny said, *"Because he is a grumpy bastard."*

Rob explained, *"My son was all I cared about. It was a kick in the guts. That day I DECIDED to change."*

In a Nutshell

Rob changed. You can change.
You are a human being. You are not a tree.

HAPPY PEOPLE FIND REASONS TO STAY HAPPY
ANGRY PEOPLE FIND REASONS TO STAY ANGRY

WE SEE THE WORLD AS WE ARE.

Fiona's Note

Fiona wrote to me:

> Hi Andrew, I just wanted to say a massive thank you.
>
> When I was 18, I had been severely depressed for many years. I had made attempts to end my life, I was blocking my family out, I was on medication.
>
> I bought your book, *Being Happy!*
>
> I still remember picking it up one Christmas Day, in my dark room, curtains drawn, and my family out in the lounge room celebrating.
>
> I began to read your book, and so many things began to "click" for me. The biggest was that **being happy is a choice**.
>
> I put the book down and said to myself, *"I'm so sick of feeling like this – miserable, missing out on life."*

I got up, I opened my curtains, went out and sat with my family and laughed the hardest that I have laughed in years. And from that day on I woke up every day and made a conscious effort with my thoughts and my feelings. I was choosing to be happy. I had my good and bad days, but slowly each day got easier and easier. Here I am now, 30 and very happy – and healthy mentally. Your book changed my path.

So HOW Do We Change?

Rob and Fiona are proof that we can choose a better life.

Many people hope to FIND happiness and don't. That may be the problem – expecting to just FIND it. Because happy people don't just FIND happiness. They DO certain things:

- They look for REASONS TO BE GRATEFUL.
- They have PURPOSE.
- They are KIND TO OTHERS.
- They are KIND TO THEMSELVES.

This means happiness is NOT something that just happens. We CREATE it.

Ups and Downs

No one is happy all the time. We all have ups and downs. Some days you feel more excited or more worried or more lonely or more loved.

But let's imagine you did a few simple things. Imagine you:

- complained less
- stopped criticising yourself
- began to focus on what you are proud of
- spent more time around people who make you happy.

What would happen?

Your GOOD DAYS WOULD GET BETTER and YOUR BAD DAYS WOULD GET BETTER.

You would still have UPS and DOWNS, but now your bad days would be manageable, and your good days would be really good.

Be Kind to Yourself

Here are four ways you can be kinder to yourself.

1. Stop Complaining!

Some people complain constantly about their illness or their boss. Some people complain about everything.

What is the problem with complaining?

When you TALK about things that upset you, you THINK more about things that upset you. For example, every time you talk about your rude neighbour, you think about him. So YOU MAKE YOURSELF unhappy!

So, complaining for the sake of complaining is a bad idea.

Obviously, if you are fixing a problem, you may need to discuss it with someone who can help, and that's different.

But telling everyone you didn't sleep last night or grumbling about the weather? Bad idea. It hurts you – and it hurts the people who have to listen to you.

Who – and what – can you quit complaining about?

For the next week, try this: *NO COMPLAINING!*

Whenever you catch yourself complaining, STOP or change the subject.

2. Support Yourself

Criticising yourself never helps. Dr Russ Harris, author of *The Reality Slap*, gives this example. I use *my words* to explain *his idea*:[4]

Imagine that you need to choose a friend to join you on a difficult journey. You can choose **Friend A** who will criticise you, and tell you, *"You'll never make it! You are pathetic. You are a loser. You've done a lot of bad things."*

Or you can choose **Friend B** who will encourage you, and tell you, *"I believe in you. It's okay to be nervous. You have a lot to be proud of."*

Which friend would be more helpful? A or B?

Obviously, B.

So what kind of friend should you be to yourself? A or B? What kind of self-talk will bring out the best in you?

When you are really ready to be happier, you make more positive choices.

*Maybe you **eat better** or **exercise more**.*

*You **complain less**.*

*You look for reasons to **be grateful**.*

And life gets better.

*Which means **happiness begins as a decision**.*

Some of us have been criticised our whole lives. We had teachers telling us, "*You're lazy!*", a dad who said, "*You should be more like your brother!*" and a mum who said, "*You should have married someone else!*"

No wonder we criticise ourselves!

But for your life to get better – and for people to treat you better – you must be kind to yourself.

For the next week: NO CRITICISING YOURSELF! Look only for good things in yourself.

You say, "What about my self-critical thoughts?" We'll get to that.

Bouncing Back

Why be kind to ourselves? Life treats us as we treat us.

3. Be Proud!

When Wimbledon champions walk on court, they're thinking about the best matches they ever played. When great entertainers walk onstage, they're thinking about how well they can sing.

Top performers have a video library in their head of proud moments.

But what do we sometimes focus on? Where we failed.

"I should have got that job!"
"I shouldn't have screwed up!"

What are YOU proud of? For example, did you ever:

- persist in a tough job
- get promoted
- earn a degree
- beat an addiction
- learn a language
- bounce back from a relationship break-up
- raise a family
- forgive somebody
- help a friend?

Did you ever accept a challenge and surprise yourself?

Make a list. Add to it. Put your list in your journal, in your drawer or pin it by your desk.

Remind yourself regularly what you are proud of. It gives you confidence. It improves your performance.

4. Connect with Positive People

Did you ever race into a public toilet that smelled so bad you wanted to choke? But you hung in there because you had to finish what you started.

Did you notice something? By the time you left five minutes later, it didn't smell quite as bad.

And what if you had accidentally locked yourself in there for an hour? You might be saying, *"Smells fine!"*

There's a principle operating here. We adapt to our environment! People who live near train stations don't hear the trains.

If you hang out with miserable people, at first you think, "*These people are so unhappy!*" Gradually, they drag you down. Misery becomes normal.

Work with critical people, and you become critical, and you think it's normal.

YOU **BECOME** LIKE THE PEOPLE YOU MIX WITH. SEEK OUT PEOPLE WHO ARE **GENEROUS, MOTIVATED** AND **HAPPY.**

Mix with lazy people, and lazy becomes normal.

Mix with happy and motivated people, and you become happy and motivated – and you think that's normal.

We are all affected and infected by the people around us. You need friends who are generous, motivated and happy.

Are you surrounded by negative people at work? In the short term, you probably need your job to pay the rent. But in the long term, you need to be around quality people – and this may mean a different job.

You owe it to yourself.

Do you live with people who are negative and unhappy? If so, you need to balance the time you spend with them, with time spent with uplifting people.

We Are Affected by the Company We Keep

Fred says, "I have these lazy friends, but they don't affect me. I have these negative friends, but they don't affect me..."

Don't kid yourself, Fred! We are all influenced by the people around us.

You need a plan to connect with positive people.

Who do you need to see more often? Who can you call once a week, once a month, who will uplift you?

Decide to find more people like them.

Alf

When Alf was ten years old he was knocked off his bicycle by a drunk driver. Alf spent nine months in hospital, nearly died, lost a leg and was paralysed from the neck down.

Imagine spending 54 years in a wheelchair because of a stranger's carelessness.

Alf had a fruit stall at our local "Rusty's" farmers' market. He sold papayas, mangoes and lychees. He was always respectful and kind. He always had a smile – whether you bought his fruit or not.

He loved growing things, writing, fishing, talking football. He never stopped learning.

Alf started an association to help disabled people. He was active in spinal research. He married twice, and raised three children.

In 20 years, I never once heard Alf complain.

Alf passed away at 64. And Alf's funeral? It is the biggest funeral I have ever attended.

There was standing room only in the chapel. There were people crowded outside at every window. There were rows of chairs on the veranda and not a spare seat. And there were three tents on the lawn, each with standing room only!

We celebrated the life of a humble man who had a little fruit stall at the farmers' market.

Would you like to live an extraordinary life?

This was Alf's way:

- Don't complain.
- Focus on what you have.
- Find a way to help someone.

"I Would Be Happy If…"

"We aren't very good at figuring out what will make us happy!"

Professor Dan Gilbert

What makes us different from dogs? We can *imagine* the future. We *imagine* things that would make us happy. Dogs don't.

Dogs don't say, *"If I could lose five kilos I could like myself."* Dogs don't say, *"I would be happy if I was in Hawaii."*

Good or Bad?

We imagine **good fortune**, like winning the lottery. We say, *"That would make me happy!"*

We can imagine **misfortune**, like a car accident, and being confined to a wheelchair, like Alf. Most people would say, *"That would be terrible!"*

Which would you choose: the money or the accident?

Is this a silly question?

Professor Gilbert of Harvard University collected data on two groups of people:
- Group A: lottery winners
- Group B: people who became paraplegics due to an accident.

Each group rated their happiness one year after the event.

So how do you think these two groups rated their own happiness?
- Group A: maybe 70% or 80% happy?
- Group B: maybe 30% or 40% happy?

The actual data: **BOTH groups rated themselves about 50% happy!**

Says Professor Gilbert, "*A year after winning the lottery and a year after losing the use of their legs, lottery winners and paraplegics are equally happy with their lives.*"[5]

Isn't that amazing? This kind of data confirms two things:

- **Regardless of EVENTS, we return to our usual happiness level.** People who experience life-changing events – like a lottery win or serious accident – return to their usual happiness level within about five weeks.
- **It's not EVENTS that make us happy.** It's how we process the events. We think that marriage, a promotion, or parenthood will change everything. The things that we think will have a huge effect on our happiness, often don't!

How Can This Be?

Psychologists explain that we have a *happiness set point*.

Your air conditioner has a *set point*, controlled by a thermostat. Regardless of the weather outside, the temperature inside your room remains fairly constant.

We are similar. Regardless of external events, the happiness level inside our heads remains fairly constant.

*ORDINARY people say,
"When I am HAPPY.
then I'll be GRATEFUL."*

*EXTRAORDINARY people say,
"When I am GRATEFUL.
then I'll be HAPPY."*

"A Pay Rise Would Make Me Happy!"

You may say, *"But a pay rise would make me happy!"*

It would! Research tells us you would be happier – for about two weeks.

You get a 5% pay rise. You are thrilled. You buy a better car. You soon adjust to the bigger pay packet. Within two weeks your happiness level is back to normal.

Then you discover that your colleague got a 10% pay rise! Now you are angry!

We think, *"When my circumstances improve – when I have more money, when my boss changes his attitude, when my kids are grateful... I'll be happy."* Not necessarily.

In a Nutshell

*It's not what happens to you that creates your happiness.
It's not even what you achieve that creates your happiness.*

It's how you think.

How Do Happy People Think?

What is one big difference between happy people and unhappy people? GRATITUDE.

Happy people CELEBRATE what they have.

Why does gratitude matter?

Because you can't be grateful AND miserable at the same time. You can't be grateful AND angry at the same time. Try it.

There will always be things "missing" from your life. You may have:

- difficult parents
- colleagues who do less than they should
- less money than you need
- neighbours who play loud music at 3.00 am.

No one's life is perfect. So how to find peace of mind?

Your happiness depends on the questions you ask yourself, for example:

- *"What do I like about my job?"*
- *"What do I love about my family, my town, my country?"*
- *"What was one good thing that happened today?"*

When you look for good things, you FIND more good things AND you begin to ATTRACT good people and more opportunities.

Life gets better. This means that a better life doesn't start in the outside world. A better life starts in your head.

GRATITUDE:
EVERY TIME YOU SAY
A SILENT *"THANK YOU"*
YOU BECOME MORE
PEACEFUL AND
MORE **POWERFUL**.

The Benefits of Gratitude

We know that anger and resentment can make you sick. So, what does gratitude do?

1. **Gratitude reduces stress** – so you have more energy.
2. **Gratitude produces chemicals in your brain** – dopamine and serotonin – which make you happier.
3. **These happy chemicals reduce pain.** That's good!
4. **Gratitude helps you sleep better.**

Gratitude: it beats being angry!

"Where Do I Start?"

You say, "How do I start to make my life better?"

- *"Should I change my husband?"*
- *"Should I change my job?"*
- *"Should I move to the Bahamas?"*

You can start with something easier. Here's what can be helpful: writing a gratitude list.

How to Make a Gratitude List

Make a little list every day of what you are grateful for. List at least three things.

You can write your list in a diary or a journal. You can use the PDF that you can download here: www.andrewmatthews.com/list

Or you can use your phone to create your gratitude list. There are dozens of phone apps to choose from. It's amazing how many people make gratitude lists and keep gratitude journals.

Why a Gratitude List?

Why have a simple daily practice of looking for good things? Because it reprograms your mind.

You may say, "*I did it once – for a week.*" Perfect. Continue!

Why do we write things down? Because writing things has more impact.

Make your list at the same time each day. You are more likely to remember if you do it first thing in the morning or last thing at night.

"What if I run out of things to be grateful for?"

You'll notice something about happy people: little things give them joy. They can appreciate a tiny flower. They can be thrilled by a phone call from a friend.

This means you don't need BIG items on your list.

As you appreciate more and more little things, you begin to think like happy people think.

A gratitude list changes your focus. You say, "*Will it change my life?*" Perhaps by 1% today and 1% tomorrow. In three months, that's a lot!

Bouncing Back

Your mission for the next 30 days: list three things you're grateful for every day. Make a start today.

"This Is the Last Time"

I sometimes play a game with myself: "*Imagine this is the last time*".

I imagine today's coffee is **the last** coffee I will ever drink.

I imagine this is **the last** time I will ever see the moon. I want to remember every detail, how it floats behind the clouds and reflects on the water.

I imagine this is **the last** time I will hear my wife's voice.

When I play the game, I suddenly pay attention to the moment. I discover sounds, colours, details, beauty and mystery that I would have missed, and I feel more grateful.

Try it. Next time you take a shower or stroke a dog, imagine it's the last time. Try breathing as if you are taking your last breaths.

We take so many simple things for granted. Were you ever constipated? Then you know.

Worst Day Ever

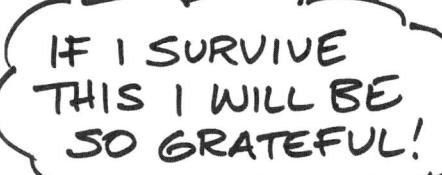

Were you ever in a bad situation, and you said to yourself, *"If I survive this, I will be so grateful"*?

Alan and Joan lived the good life in Orlando, Florida. They loved their jobs. They travelled.

Alan was a manager with a national restaurant chain. On the morning of March 19, 2007, Alan was in his home office and took a call from work.

"We're downsizing. Your position has been eliminated. Nothing personal."

Alan was jobless, just like that! He and Joan wondered, *"How will we pay the mortgage? Will we lose our home?"*

Joan went to work that day as usual.

She was a healthy 42-year-old runner, but she had recently had some medical tests. She got a call from her surgeon. He said, *"It's lymphoma. You have cancer."*

Alan was sacked, and Joan discovered she had cancer, all in one day.

That night, not knowing how they would manage – or survive – Alan said to Joan, *"Some time in the future we are going to write about today, and we'll call it Worst Day Ever."*

Alan began job hunting, calling every contact he knew. Joan found an oncologist. It turned out that Joan's cancer was slow-moving and manageable.

Some months later, Alan got a good job with another restaurant chain. Life got better.

On March 19, 2008, the first anniversary of their *Worst Day Ever*, they celebrated. They flew to Las Vegas.

Every year, Alan and Joan celebrate *Worst Day Ever*. On their 10th anniversary, they went to Ireland. They celebrate to remind themselves, "*We can get through anything!*"[6]

Entitlement

If the happiest people are the most grateful – and small things make them happy – which people are the most miserable?

Entitled people! People who believe, "*The world owes me.*"

You probably know some people like this. They act like, "*I deserve special treatment.*"

They want it all. They want it now. They only show up for work when they feel like it.

Entitlement is the fast track to misery.

In a Nutshell

When you are grateful, anything is a bonus. When you feel entitled, nothing is ever enough.

NEGATIVE THOUGHTS ARE LIKE RATS
They arrive in groups... One rat shows up and before you know it, they have taken over!

How Do I Control My Thoughts?

You have about 50,000 thoughts per day. Some are happy thoughts, such as *"This is a beautiful song!"* or *"I love my dog!"* Some are disturbing thoughts, such as *"I'm so stupid"* or *"I'm a bad person."*

Your passing thoughts are just passing traffic. You don't need to argue with them. Why get tangled up with disturbing thoughts when you can just let them go?

Just as the passing cars are **not the highway**, your thoughts **are not you**. They are just thoughts.

You say, *"So if I don't ARGUE with negative thoughts, what do I do with them?"* You REPLACE them.

"How Do I Replace Negative Thoughts?"

You are driving home, and you get stuck in a traffic jam. Your first negative thought is: *"This is the LAST THING I need!"*

Then you get a **second** negative thought: *"And I'm already LATE!"*

And a **third** negative thought: *"My WORK is stressing me out."* And a **fourth**: *"And I've got all these BILLS to pay."* And a **fifth**: *"Nobody cares about MY problems!"*

Followed by:

6: "Tonight I have to cook dinner for the family."
7: "And vacuum the house."
8: "No one appreciates me!"
9: "And I've got a HEADACHE."
10: "Maybe it's a TUMOUR!"

Is this familiar? One negative thought attracts another. A lone rat becomes a plague!

You need an extermination strategy, and this is how you rid yourself of the rats. The moment you get your first negative thought, you ask yourself:

"*What's good about being stuck in traffic?*" You may decide:

- "*I can listen to my favourite music.*"
- "*I can plan my weekend.*"
- "*It's better than walking!*"

Now you may say, "*Let's be realistic.*"

HERE'S REALISTIC:

1. Lousy things happen.
2. Resilient people have the habit of saying, "*What's good about this?*"

EXAMPLE: You are short of money. You are falling into that negative spiral. You ask yourself, "*What's GOOD about having no cash?*"

You may decide:

- "*I am learning to budget.*"
- "*It makes me more determined to succeed.*"
- "*I am learning who my friends are!*"
- "*I'll have a story to tell my grandchildren.*"

EXAMPLE: Your relationship breaks up. "*What's good about this?*"

- "*I will need to meet some new people.*"
- "*I will get out of my comfort zone.*"

When someone lets you down, when your plans get cancelled, when you miss out on a promotion, ask yourself, "*What's good about this?*" You can always find something because YOU FIND

IN LIFE WHAT YOU LOOK FOR. Find one thing to be happy about, and you break the cycle – and soon you are feeling better.

Bouncing Back

Before the rat plague starts, ask yourself, "What's good about this?" The good news? One positive thought attracts another.

Two Women Bounce Back

Chloe

Chloe and her husband, Peter, had been married for 15 years. They had two children. They worked in average jobs and lived in an ordinary apartment. They were unhappy.

They hardly spoke to each other. They were two strangers living in one home.

Then Chloe discovered Peter was having an affair with his secretary. Chloe flew into a blind rage. There were screaming matches, accusations, sleepless nights, and tears.

She threw him out.

A string of angry text messages followed, and more arguments and tears. More sleepless nights.

Six months later, Chloe was chatting with an old friend. He asked her a question that stopped her in her tracks, *"Chloe, would you want to be married to you?"*

There was a long silence. Chloe said, *"Hell, no!"*

For the first time, Chloe realised she was half the problem.

Chloe and Peter began to speak by phone. They patched things up. He moved back in. Three years on, Chloe says, *"We have our challenges, but we are happier than we ever were."*

Tina

Tina and Eric were married with two girls. He ran a small business. She worked in the city.

They were comfortable in their big home. They drove nice cars and took luxury vacations.

Her life revolved around the children: cooking their meals, delivering them to school, soccer practice, sleepovers. His life was all about work, watching football and getting drunk.

They hardly spoke to each other. They were two strangers living in one home.

Says Tina, *"I could have been on fire and Eric would never have noticed. We were both miserable. After 16 years I took the girls and left."*

Tina now lives in a small, rented apartment. She works two jobs. No fancy car. No more luxury vacations.

Four years on, Tina says, *"It's tough but I am proud of the new life we have created. The girls are settled. I should have left ten years earlier."*

So What is the Solution?

One woman patched things up and now she is happier. One woman got divorced and now she is happier. So what is the point here?

- Someone else's solution may not be your solution.
- There is always hope. Life can be better.

Resilience

How do we get physically fit? By running uphill, by resisting gravity.

How do we get mentally fit? By bouncing back from failure and disappointment.

Happiness is a sign of mental toughness.

Unlike what some people may believe, HAPPINESS is not a sign of IGNORANCE. It's a sign of RESILIENCE.

You ask, *"So do happy people wake up every morning and count their blessings?"*

Lots do!

Happy people EXPECT to find good things all around them.

They automatically ask themselves, *"What do I like about my bed, my breakfast, the weather, my work, my books, my friends, my neighbours, my coffee?"*

Here is a good thing to do before you get out of bed.

Be grateful that you woke up. "I have another day!"

EVERY MORNING WHEN YOU OPEN YOUR EYES LOOK FOR ONE REASON TO BE HAPPY.

ONE DAY AT A TIME

HOW DO YOU SURVIVE WHEN LIFE GETS TOUGH - WHEN YOU ARE WORRIED OR SCARED?

ALL YOU CAN DO IS GIVE YOUR BEST EFFORT UNTIL BEDTIME.

LET TOMORROW TAKE CARE OF ITSELF.

4

LIVE ONE DAY AT A TIME

Feeling Overwhelmed?

**Refuse to worry about what you can't fix today.
Just give your best until bedtime.**

Turia's Story

"*I used to focus on just getting through one day at a time, and when I got through one day, I'd pat myself on the back, and I'd say, 'Well done, Turia. You've made it through another day.'*

"*And then, when a day was too hard, I'd break it up into hours.*"

In 2011, Turia Pitt was running in an ultramarathon in outback Australia when an out-of-control bushfire swept across the course. Turia was trapped. She suffered burns to 65% of her body.

It was hours before medical help arrived. Doctors gave Turia no chance of survival.

Turia was placed in a medically induced coma for a month. She was in and out of hospital for two years. She had to wear a full-body compression suit and wear a face mask for 23 hours a day.

She underwent over 200 operations.

All fingers on her right hand and two fingers on her left hand had to be amputated.

Doctors told her, "*You may never run again.*"

Turia recalls, "*I couldn't brush my hair. I couldn't wipe my arse. I had to find the strength within me to bend my elbow to feed myself.*"

Turia bounced back. She walked. She ran. She surfs and sails.

In 2016 she competed in her first Ironman Australia competition. Later that year she competed in the Ironman World Championships in Hawaii.

Turia is a popular motivational speaker, she's written three best-selling books, coached 40,000 people online and raised millions of dollars for charity.

Four years after the accident, Turia had her first son with Michael Hoskin, her high school sweetheart. Now they are the proud parents of two boys.

Turia says, *"I am really proud of not only how I handled myself but how I was able to rebuild my life to a spot where I think it's even better than it was before.*

"I just focus on consistency and DOING THE SMALL THINGS THAT I CAN DO EVERY DAY that get me closer to where I want to be."

And Michael? He was so inspired by the helicopter pilot who risked his life to save Turia that he became a helicopter pilot.

WORRYING HELPS NO ONE.
Worrying attracts misfortune and it makes you sick.

Take **action** and postpone **worry**. You'll be happier and healthier.

Ummi's Story

I received a Facebook message from Ummi Abdullah, in Singapore. She said, "I was broke, my husband, my children and I were living with my parents. And I was sick.

"I went to the doctor – and on the table in the waiting room was your book, **Being Happy!**

Start anywhere you can. Give your best shot at whatever is in front of you and opportunity will begin to find you.

It's called, "Developing a reputation."

"I got to read seven pages before the doctor called me in. I had to finish the book. So I borrowed $20 to buy my own copy."

Ummi had to borrow the $20 because she was $100,000 in debt.

She said, "*Being Happy!* changed my thinking and my outlook.

"I saw an ad on Facebook – somebody wanted to pay $30 for 10 serves of chicken rice. I spent $50 on ingredients – and got back $30!"

But she said, "I was on my way. I began cooking for other people in the tiny kitchen of our apartment."

Ummi got more and more orders. She rented a commercial kitchen. Then she opened a restaurant.

Ummi bounced back. She paid off her debt. Today she owns a food and beverage company that includes a bakery.

Julie and I joined her for dinner at her restaurant, *Noosh Noodle Bar and Grill*, on the Singapore Esplanade.

How did Ummi go from a big debt to where she is now?

She started small.

In a Nutshell

Start wherever you can with whatever you have.

Anna's Story

My sister, Jane, had five children under 12 when she was diagnosed with breast cancer. She had chemotherapy, radiation and a mastectomy.

Jane was still recovering when her daughter, Anna, was in a car accident. Anna was taken to emergency by helicopter. When Anna woke from her coma, she was paralysed – unable to move, eat or speak.

Says Jane, *"My husband Steve and I knew that our lives had changed forever."*

After 20 months in hospital, Anna still could not move even a finger. Anna was fed through a tube. Jane and Steve took her home to care for her at home.

In 2006 they took Anna to China for stem cell therapy. It didn't really help.

Says Jane, *"After about five years I began to accept that there wasn't going to be any miracle cure and I stopped being so desperate. I still cry."*

Acceptance

Twenty years later, Anna is still unable to move.

Says Jane, *"We have lived a normal life and raised four other children. We are a happy family. We have had a lot of help in caring for Anna – for that we are so grateful.*

"What's most important? Acceptance. Whatever happens, we deal with it one day at a time."

24 Hours Only

Imagine that for no particular reason, you collected everything you need to eat in the next five years – and all the clothes you need to wear in the next five years – and you **carried it all around on your BACK.**

How would that work for you?

You would collapse!

You aren't designed to carry that kind of load.

But you can carry what you need for **24 hours**.

Your Worries

Okay, so imagine that you made a list of everything that you need TO DO over the next five years, and everything that could GO WRONG over the next five years, and you **carried it all around in your HEAD**: the stock market might collapse, you might catch malaria or bird flu, you might get the sack or be kidnapped by terrorists or...

You could go nuts.

You aren't designed to carry that kind of load.

You are perfectly designed to live life in 24-hour compartments.

Your PRESENT MOMENTS are mostly bearable.

It's the FUTURE that drives you nuts. And your life is simply a series of present moments, all of which you have survived.

So tell yourself, *"I will deal with tomorrow when I get there!"*

You can handle one day at a time.

Some people will tell you, *"You SHOULD worry!"*

But worrying is WORSE THAN USELESS!

Firstly, it attracts misfortune. Secondly, it is bad for your health!

So what should you do about worry? Postpone it!

Take action FIRST. Postpone worry indefinitely.

Do whatever you can do today – and leave worry out of it.

Step by Step

Tackle your problems as you would climb a mountain.

If you go rock climbing, and you get stuck on a ledge, you suddenly focus on the present moment!

When your life is in danger, you forget about the future. All your effort goes into your next step.

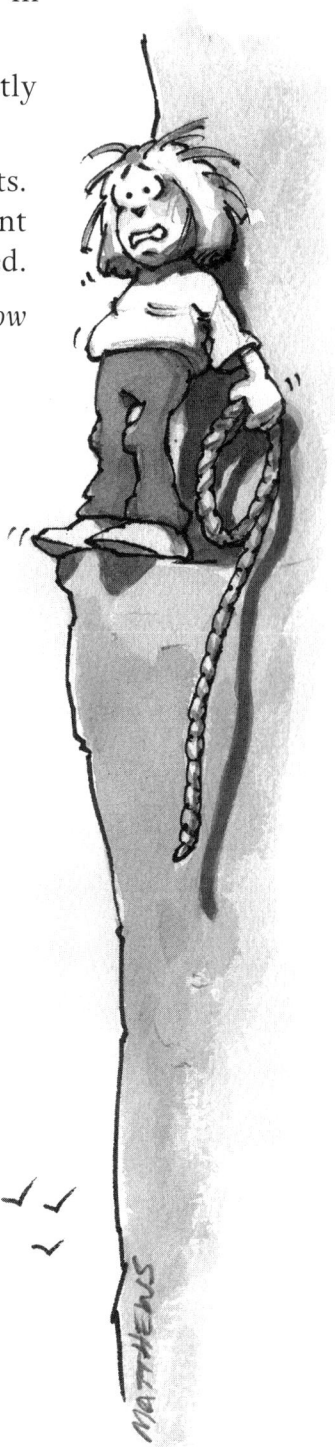

Then your next step. Inch by inch. Eventually, you claw your way out.

The same strategy works for everyday life.

You say, *"How can I stay positive when I can't even pay the rent?"* *"How do I keep going when I'm grieving, lonely or seriously ill?"*

When the worst happens, you can't worry about the rest of your life. You can't even be worrying about the rest of the month. All you can do is do your best right now.

In a Nutshell

Tell yourself each day, "I will do my best until bedtime – and when tomorrow comes, I will deal with it."

And whenever 24 hours is too tough, bite off five minutes at a time.

Feeling Overwhelmed?

Too much to do? Write a list of everything you need to do. You'll feel better already.

Tomorrow, do the five most important things. Next day, update the list and do the five most important things.

Repeat. You feel better when you have a plan.

Small Steps

Research confirms that you are more likely to tackle jobs that you can complete in 15 minutes or less. So when you make your list, break the bigger tasks into small steps.

How to Get Better at Anything

David Rush holds the world record for blowing up the most balloons in one minute with his nose. (It's ten balloons.) You can try this at home. You can try this at home – and you need to tie the knot in each balloon.

David holds the world record for balancing a lawn mower on his chin: 30 minutes and 33 seconds.

He is also the world's fastest man at running 100 metres while juggling blindfolded!

David has broken over 200 world records.

You say, *"David, WHY?"*

David is an educator. For David it's about learning new skills and having fun. He says: *"EVEN IF YOU ARE NOT GOOD WHEN YOU START, YOU CAN BECOME THE BEST IN THE WORLD."*

As a kid, David was always picked last for ball games. He grew up doubting himself.

This is his message to young people:

"If you believe in yourself, if you set yourself a goal and pursue it, you can accomplish almost anything – including breaking world records.

"You can become better at anything."

You may never need to balance a lawnmower on your face. But you may want to get better at managing people or driving a truck or giving speeches.

When Your Friends Say, *"That's Too Difficult!"*

When I was 45, I began studying Mandarin. Friends warned me, *"It's really hard!"*

I had learnt about six words when I was booked to give a 90-minute speech in Beijing, in English, with a translator.

The Beijing conference was more than eight months away. So I had time to prepare. I thought, *"I already know six words! Maybe I should give my presentation in Chinese!"*

I wrote my speech in English and counted the sentences: there were 510. I figured, *"If I learn two Chinese sentences by heart each day for 255 days, I can probably do it!"*

My Mandarin teacher, Wanyi, kindly translated my talk, and I began studying my two sentences per day. I was up at 4.30 every morning, studying. It was harder than I expected!

I learned 62 Chinese sentences the first month, and kept at it, two sentences per day.

Finally, after eight months, I got to 500. And would you believe it? On the morning that I learned sentence number 508, the conference was cancelled!

A few months later I gave that presentation in Singapore, in Chinese. It wasn't perfect. I was happy. And I did better the next time.

In a Nutshell

Whatever you want to do – even if your friends say, "It's too hard!" or "You are too old!" – break it into small chunks. You may surprise yourself.

The secret: PRACTISE EVERY DAY. The lesson: TODAY MATTERS.

Make a Start

In physics we learn about momentum: it is more difficult to get something moving than to keep it moving. For example:

In a rowboat, the hardest bit is rowing the FIRST ten metres. In business: the hardest bit is making your FIRST $1,000.

Success is about momentum. We talk about people being "on a roll!"

The key is to make a start. So if you want to:

GET FIT: If all you can run is 50 metres, run those 50 metres!
SAVE MONEY: If all you can save is $5, save that $5!

CLEAN YOUR OFFICE: If you have time to tidy just one drawer, tidy that drawer.

If someone is offering you a job, and it's the only job offer you have, grab it, learn all you can, get some confidence, gather momentum.

In a Nutshell

If you can succeed a little bit, success will tend to continue.

**YOU DON'T HAVE TO BE *GREAT* TO *START*
BUT YOU HAVE TO *START* TO BE *GREAT*.**

Zig Ziglar

Finding the Energy

Did you ever tell yourself:
"I will exercise when I get the energy."
"I will tidy my bedroom when I get motivated."

Here's the point:
You find the energy AFTER you begin.
You gather momentum AFTER you begin.

Lana

Lana owns a local hairdressing salon. She cuts my hair.

About 40 haircuts ago, she told me, "*I am in my thirties, with three kids. My husband and I have never saved, we have never owned a home, and we are $18,000 in debt!*"

Lana said, "*We have started saving for a home. I quit buying café lattes and bottled water. I now make my lunch.*

"*We live on a strict budget. If something is beyond the budget, we don't buy it. We have a special savings account, and we save every week!*"

About 25 haircuts later she proudly announced, "*We have paid off our $18,000 debt, we saved a $10,000 deposit and bought a home!*" Because her parents guaranteed the loan, the bank required only a small deposit.

It took Lana and her husband almost three years to pay off their debt and save the deposit. You might say, "*That's a long time!*" But whether you save your money or not, *the three years will go by anyway.*

In a Nutshell

Do you need money for something? Make a start. Today matters.

Ross Edgley

Ross Edgley likes to test his limits.

Ross was training for a marathon swim in tropical Bermuda when his good friend, Ollie, said, "*Why don't you do something really amazing? Why don't you swim around GREAT BRITAIN?*"

Ross thought, "*That's a good idea!*"

Friends told Ross, "*It's impossible.*" So Ross consulted a sports laboratory to ask the experts:

    A: "*Is it humanly possible?*" and

    B: "*Is it possible for Ross Edgley?*"

The laboratory spent hours testing Ross and delivered their verdict.

They said, "*Ross, you are TOO SHORT, you have the WRONG BODY SHAPE, you have NO FAT TO KEEP YOU AFLOAT and NO FAT TO KEEP YOU WARM! Your HEAD IS TOO BIG AND TOO HEAVY. You are a HUMAN SUBMARINE!*"

They concluded, "*Ross, YOU ARE THE LAST PERSON TO BE SWIMMING AROUND THE UK! The only thing you have going for you is that you have childbearing hips.*"

With this encouragement, on June 1, 2018, Ross jumped into the sea at Margate and began swimming clockwise around Great Britain.

Ross was wearing a brand-new wetsuit.

New wetsuits are like new shoes – they are stiff and they wear holes in your flesh. By the end of day one, Ross had a huge gash in his neck that got worse.

Ross kept swimming with a hole in his neck.

He swam for 12 hours a day, battling powerful tides, huge waves, freezing cold, oil tankers, shocking pollution, sea lice, sea sickness, giant jellyfish and a body that ached to quit.

After 157 days and 1780 miles and no sick days, Ross swam back into Margate.

Says Ross, "*When your mind is telling you that you are done, that you're exhausted, that you cannot possibly go any further, you're only actually 40% done.*"

You might say, "*Should I be inspired? He's nuts!*"

Here's what you might also say: "*If Ross Edgley can SWIM around England, Wales and Scotland, I can DRIVE to the gym.*"[7]

In a Nutshell

We can do extraordinary things, one day at a time.

THE GREAT BRITISH SWIM

Khaby Lame

He's famous. He makes people laugh. He makes millions. How lucky was Khaby Lame?

Khaby's family migrated from Senegal to Italy. They were poor, and Khaby is dyslexic. He struggled at school. So Khaby found work in a factory and as a waiter. When COVID hit, Khaby lost BOTH jobs.

With no money and no work, Khaby decided, *"I want to make people laugh."* He began posting on TikTok.

After one month he had TWO followers; his father and a neighbour. In one whole month he got nine views!

It didn't worry Khaby. He kept posting his little videos, one after another. Within two years, Khaby went from two followers to two hundred million.

That's how Khaby Lame became the face of *Hugo Boss*.

Bouncing Back

Says Khaby, "You must keep doing what you want. Other people might say 'It's impossible.' But those are their limits, not yours."

"Don't judge each day by the harvest you reap but by the seeds you plant."

Robert Louis Stevenson

Success Is Not about Brilliance

In real life, you discover that:

- university professors were mostly just average students
- successful entrepreneurs went broke and bounced back
- the greatest sporting champions were not the most talented teenagers.

You think success is about IQ and TALENT?

Here's what really matters: PERSISTENCE and RESILIENCE. Everyone has setbacks and disappointments.

HIGH ACHIEVERS OFTEN START FROM FAR BEHIND

Asthmatics become Olympians. Bankrupts become billionaires. Refugees become university professors.

The mental toughness you develop just to survive becomes your secret weapon.

Tom Brady

"People didn't think I'd play one year in the NFL."

Tom Brady became one of American football's greatest quarterbacks and surprised a lot of people.

In the draft of 2000, Tom was repeatedly ignored by every professional team in the country before being picked 199th by the New England Patriots.

Tom wasn't quite strong enough. He wasn't quite fast enough. Nothing about him was extraordinary – except his extraordinary work ethic: *Train harder than anyone, refine your skills, never stop learning.*

In a game where most quarterbacks last for four seasons, Brady played for 23. He won a record seven Super Bowl titles and was named the game's Most Valuable Player five times.

Rock Stars

You say, "Maybe great footballers work hard, but what about rock stars? What if you're the Rolling Stones?"

Keith Richards explained, *"The reason our concerts are seamless is that, before we go on tour, we practise 14 hours a day."*

LIFE REWARDS EFFORT, NOT EXCUSES.

Red Hot Chili Peppers' lead guitarist, John Frusciante, practises for four hours before a concert.

His bandmate, Flea, explained his injured thumb from practising bass guitar, *"I did this so much and so aggressively that this callous in my thumb was split open. I had this gash – this open wound in my thumb. And I figured out how to fix it by pouring super glue in there."*

How do the *Red Hot Chili Peppers* still fill stadiums after 40 years?

Says Flea, *"It takes diligence. It takes sacrifice. We work, we write, we never stop. This is our purpose. We're humble. We are students. We care. We want to grow. We want to learn."*

In a Nutshell

The myth is that achievers are outrageously lucky or outrageously talented. Even rock stars are outrageously committed.

Have a Plan

I often present to high schools. I say to students, *"Let's say you want to be a pilot. You need to pass mathematics to be a pilot and you are failing mathematics.*

"Does that mean you can't be a pilot? NO!

"You make a plan to study an extra hour of maths every day.

"By next month you are probably still failing! But in three months you are doing better. In six months you are getting good grades. In a year, you're at the top of the class.

"Now your friends are asking, 'How come you're so smart?'

"You don't need to be brilliant. But you do need a plan. How do you improve at anything? One bite at a time. One day at a time."

Akash Karia

Akash Karia sent me an email: *"I attended your talk at the University of Science and Technology in Hong Kong in 2005.*

"After your presentation, I joined the queue of people who were buying your books. I couldn't afford a book, but I stood in line anyway.

"When it was finally my turn, I asked you, 'How do you write a book?'

You gave me the best advice I ever received, 'WRITE A PAGE EVERY DAY'."

Where Is Akash Today?

What happened to the kid who couldn't afford a $20 book? Akash has written 16 books, published in six languages. Akash now has a global corporate training business.

Akash writes one page per day.

In a Nutshell

You don't need to be brilliant. You need to be consistent.

*You don't **FIND** the **PERFECT JOB**. You find a **GOOD** job and do your best every day.*

You encourage and support your colleagues. You surprise and delight your customers.

*Then one day you realise that a **GOOD** job became **WONDERFUL**.*

"How Do I Find the Perfect Job?"

There's much talk these days about *following your passion*.

Professor Shane Lopez of the University of Kansas interviewed 8,500 employees and asked:

- *"Do you love your job?"*
- *"If so, how did you find it? Did you follow your passion?"*

Of the 8,500, about 1100 said they loved their work. What did these 1100 people tell Professor Lopez?

They rarely talked of following their passion or FINDING the perfect job.

Their message was, *"I took a GOOD job and I:*

- *built relationships*
- *encouraged people*
- *made customers feel special*
- *built a team*
- *promoted kindness*
- *did my best one day after another*

and my GOOD job became WONDERFUL."[9]

Good jobs are not FOUND. They are CREATED.

Bouncing Back

It's not so much WHAT you do, as HOW you do it.

Doing Your Best

Did you ever watch a four-year-old draw a portrait of her dad? Did you ever see a brain surgeon save a life on TV, or hear a concert pianist in full flight? Did you ever watch a window cleaner polish mirrors in a hotel elevator, giving it his best effort? It is a wonderful thing.

There is something noble and uplifting about watching people doing their best.

But there is something better, and that is to BE that child, to BE that surgeon, to BE that violinist, TO BE THAT WINDOW CLEANER.

*WHY GIVE YOUR **BEST** AT **WHATEVER YOU DO?***
*BECAUSE IT IS THE **ONLY WAY** TO ENJOY YOUR WORK.*

How do you enjoy your work? Give it everything.

Miserable people do as little as possible. It is like they measure out their energy.

Fred says, *"My colleagues don't work that hard."* Not your business, Fred.
Fred says, *"But my boss doesn't appreciate me."* Irrelevant.
Fred says, *"But I am underpaid."* Irrelevant.

Your job may not be perfect. Maybe you are going to quit at five o'clock today. But here's how you feel best about you today: by giving it all you've got until five.

You don't give your best to impress your boss. You do it for you.

In a Nutshell

Often, we don't need to change our JOB. We need to change our ATTITUDE.

5

EVERYBODY FAILS

If you fall down, get back up!

How we learn.
Does it matter what other people think?

Ivan

When I was twelve, I played football for the *Encounter Bay Eagles*. I wasn't very good. My buddy, Ivan, was a star. He was "best-on-ground" almost every week. It all seemed so easy for him.

Years later, his sister told me how nervous Ivan got every Saturday. She said, *"He threw up before every game!"*

Who knew? It looked so easy for Ivan.

Some people *SEEM* to achieve overnight success!

Some couples *SEEM* to never argue!

Some people's lives *SEEM* almost perfect.

It looks good from a distance. But everyone struggles.

When you know the inside story — the struggles and disappointments — of anyone, it can break your heart.

Ted

My friend, Ted, is a joker and the life of the party.

Ted makes fun of all his mates, and his mates all make fun of Ted. Why? Because Ted always has a smart answer.

Nothing worries Ted. Or SO IT SEEMS.

Last month in a quiet moment, Ted said to me, *"Every day I worry about what people think of me. Not a day goes by that I don't ask myself, 'Have I done the right thing? Have I said the right thing?' My life is torture!"*

Ted is living a nightmare. Who would guess?

Everybody hurts, including people like Ted who seem bullet-proof.

Everybody hurts, including people you find difficult and unreasonable.

No one is as confident as they seem. Some of us grew up being told we're stupid. Some of us grew up convinced we're ugly. Some of us believe we are unlovable.

Most of us worry that we are not good enough. I do.

Being a human is hard. Everyone is hurting.

Everybody Hurts

Katy Perry failed and hurt.

Katy Perry has sold about 150 million records. With her album, *Teenage Dream*, she became only the second artist ever to land five USA number 1 hits from one album.

How many copies did her first record sell? Two hundred! And things got worse.

By the age of 23, Katy had been dumped by three record companies.

When the world finally heard Katy Perry's songs, music critics were often vicious.

If you were dumped by three record companies by the time you were 23, and if music experts were telling you to get a real job, would you want to quit?

Lionel Messi

"When you saw him you would think: this kid can't play ball. He's a dwarf, he's too fragile, too small..."

Lionel Messi's Youth Soccer Coach, Adrián Coria

Lionel was a tiny child – and shy. At ten he was diagnosed with a growth hormone disorder. He underwent years of hormone injections into his legs to help him grow. Despite the treatment, Messi remained one of the shorter players on the field.

Did it stop Lionel?

Lionel won six Golden Boots (for the European First Division's top goal scorer) and seven Ballon d'Or awards (for the world's best player).

In 2016, after Argentina suffered its third consecutive defeat in a major final, Lionel really hurt. He announced his retirement from international football. But not for long.

He bounced back! In Qatar in 2022, Lionel Messi led Argentina to win the World Cup.

You Say, "So What?"

You say, *"I've heard all these 'failure to success' stories. They're so common."* EXACTLY! Failure is everywhere!

It's YOUR story. When you were learning to walk, you fell over about 17 times an hour. That's roughly 500 times a week. Did you quit? You know about persistence.

Almost anyone who ever went to school or quit school, anyone who ever found a job, kept a job or lost a job, has failed and hurt. If you have ever been lonely, heartbroken, felt like a loser, wanted to give up, you are just like Lionel and Katy and the rest of us.

Failure: it's the story behind the books we love and the sports stars we watch.

Rafael Nadal

Tennis champion Rafael Nadal always hurts.

Nadal was hit by injuries from the age of 17. He suffered tendonitis in both knees, adductor problems, recurrent back pain, torn hamstrings, torn abdominal muscles, scaphoid stress fractures, recurrent wrist injuries and a cracked rib. Nadal also has an incurable, degenerative foot condition.

Injuries kept Nadal out of tennis for months at a time. Almost every year it seemed Nadal's career might be over. There were long periods of heartbreaking disappointment and despair.

Nadal entered the 2022 French Open suffering constant foot pain. He needed pain-killing injections just to play each match. He played through the pain.

When Nadal triumphed in the final – winning a record 14th French Open – he also broke the record at the time for the most Grand Slam singles titles for a male player.

Our Favourite Books

Dr Seuss

Dr Seuss's books, including *Green Eggs and Ham*, *Fox in Socks* and *The Cat in the Hat*, have sold over 600 million copies.

Dr Seuss's first book (his real name was Theodor Seuss Geisel) was rejected by 28 publishers before Random House said, *"Yes"*.

JK Rowling

Author JK Rowling was a single mother who could barely feed her children. She was so poor she wrote in cafes to save on heating. Her first book, *Harry Potter and the Philosopher's Stone*, was rejected 12 times.

A literary agent advised Rowling, *"You do realise you will never make a fortune out of writing children's books?"*

Rowling was diagnosed with clinical depression and underwent therapy. Then she found a small publisher.

In 2004 JK Rowling became the world's first billionaire author.

Failure, Rejection, Disaster: it's the story behind our favourite movies.

The **STAR WARS** script was rejected by United Artists, Universal and Disney. Director George Lucas was so sure it would bomb, he skipped the premiere and went to Hawaii.

TITANIC was plagued with sick actors, injured stunt people, exploding budgets and actors wanting to quit.

While shooting in Nova Scotia, somebody spiked the catered food on set. They put an hallucinogenic drug, Phencyclidine (PCP), in the lobster chowder! Cast members began hallucinating, crying and throwing up. About fifty were taken to hospital.

Nobody died, and James Cameron finished the movie.[10]

BACK to the FUTURE was rejected by 40 studios, including every major studio.

Rocky

Rocky won three Academy Awards including Best Picture. But the movie almost never happened.

Sylvester "Sly" Stallone played Rocky. He only ever wanted to be an actor.

Stallone knows about failure and hurt.

Stallone suffered nerve damage at birth. When doctors used forceps to help him down the birth canal, they severed a nerve in his cheek. Sly has no feeling in the lower left side of his face. So he can't smile, and he slurs like a drunk.

The angry kid who struggled to speak was bullied and got into fist fights. By the age of 13, Stallone had been expelled from 14 schools.

Sly studied acting in Miami and then moved to New York to find work. It's tough being an actor with a paralysed face. Sly was rejected for more than a thousand roles. Who needs a guy that can't smile and can't speak properly? He moved to Los Angeles, hoping his luck would change.

A New Strategy

Sly rented a tiny apartment, he had a broken-down $40 car, $106 in the bank and no money to feed his dog. He sold his dog to a stranger outside a 7-Eleven store for $60.

Sly decided, *"If I don't fit OTHER PEOPLE'S movies, I WILL WRITE A MOVIE SCRIPT TO FIT ME... about a guy who was knocked down but he got up."*

He wrote the rough draft of Rocky in three and a half days and shared the script with Hollywood movie people. Reactions were mixed. Some studios found it *"predictable and stupid"*. Some told him, *"Boxing movies make no money."*

"We Don't Want You!"

Stallone found two producers who loved the script. They offered $125,000.

Stallone said, *"Okay, but ONLY if I can play the lead."*
They said, *"NO, WE JUST WANT THE SCRIPT. WE DON'T WANT YOU."*
Stallone argued, *"It's my movie. I get the lead role."*

The studio wouldn't budge. They upped the offer to $250,000 and then to $350,000.

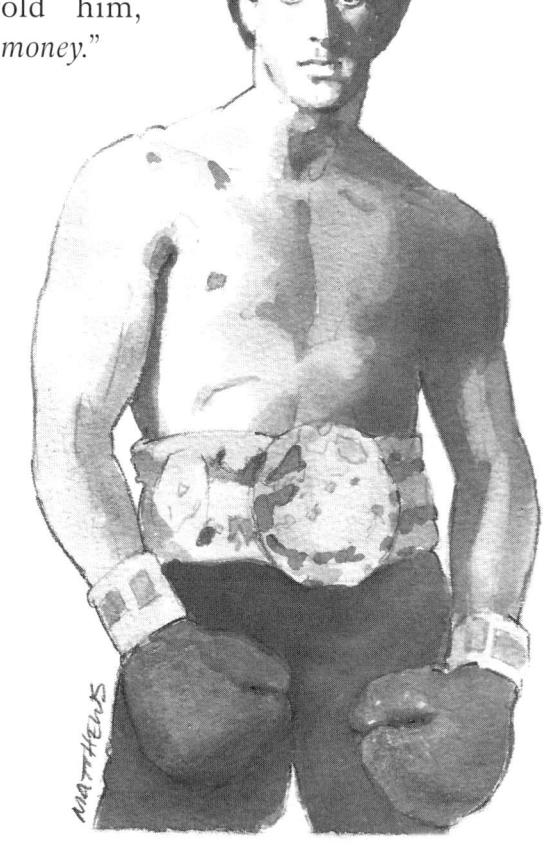

"I AM NOT THE RICHEST, SMARTEST OR MOST TALENTED PERSON IN THE WORLD BUT I SUCCEED BECAUSE I KEEP GOING AND GOING AND GOING,"

Sylvester Stallone

Says Stallone, *"They kept offering me more and more money NOT to be in my movie!"*

Stallone walked away from the $350,000 offer.

Finally, they all agreed on a deal:

- $35,000 for the script – down from $350,000!
- Stallone would get the lead role.
- a tiny budget of just a million dollars. They said, *"Why risk money on a no-name actor?"*

They shot *Rocky* in 28 days.

"I Sat There, Humiliated"

Stallone recalls the movie premiere, *"I really had no confidence. I was not a film maker. I had no history. Finally, it was being shown at the Directors Guild and this was going to be the test."*

Nine hundred people were at the premiere.

Says Stallone, *"The movie was playing terribly. The laughs weren't coming where they were supposed to. The fight itself seemed listless."*

Everyone left the theatre except for Stallone and his mother. He remembers, *"I sat there humiliated and saddened by the whole thing. I couldn't believe it. I said, 'Ma, I really blew it. It was nice while it lasted.'*

"I walked out and there were three flights of stairs: first flight, second...

"By the time I turned to the third flight, the entire audience was down there. There were 900 people waiting and they began to applaud, I mean TRULY APPLAUD!

"I completely came apart. I will never get over that moment."

Rocky became a global sensation. Five more *Rocky* movies followed.

What about His Dog?

As soon as Sly signed the movie deal, he went to the 7-Eleven to find the guy who bought his dog. After three days the guy showed up, but he wouldn't sell the dog.

Finally, the guy said, *"I'll give you the dog back for three thousand."* Sly said, *"I don't have three thousand!"*

The guy said, *"All right, I wanna be in the movie!"*

Sly took his dog and put the guy in the movie – and put his dog in the movie.

The BIG Lie

If Sly Stallone was rejected for a thousand movie parts, if Katy Perry's first album sold 200 copies, if JK Rowling was rejected by 12 publishers, HOW MUCH IS SUCCESS ABOUT TALENT?

Not that much. The world is full of talented people.

We grow up believing a lie. We imagine that our favourite artists and sporting heroes, and people like Steve Jobs or Richard Branson who changed our world, got lucky.

We like to label achievers as gifted. It can be an excuse for us not to make a bigger effort.

Why These Stories?

You say, *"I don't want to be a writer or a movie star or change the world. Why all these stories?"*

Because it helps to know how other people struggled, so that when our lives get tough, we don't feel like victims – and we don't complain, *"Life's not fair!"*

Whether you sell real estate or care for old folks, whether you fix Toyotas or fix people's teeth, you will also be challenged, let down, disappointed.

In a Nutshell

People who bounce back don't worry about whether life is fair.

It Looks Good on the Outside

We read about entrepreneurs who got rich. We hear of people like Amazon's Jeff Bezos. Maybe you went to a barbecue and met a guy whose cousin has a friend who is making millions online. It sounds easy.

But there is always a story behind the story.

We watch a breathtaking documentary about snow leopards or polar bears. What we don't know is that some guy froze in a tent for four months to shoot 20 minutes of good video.

It all looks GOOD on the OUTSIDE but sometimes it's HELL on the INSIDE.

Let's Toughen up and Get Real!

Most songs, manuscripts, musicals, and TV shows fail. Ninety percent of internet businesses fail within 120 days.

Most successful businesses almost go broke.

If you ever felt crushed, disappointed or exhausted, that's how life can be when you apply for jobs, build websites, publish videos, open cafes or look for love.

The world will test us. We all fail. It doesn't mean that there is something wrong with us or that we can't succeed.

Animals fail! When lions go deer hunting, they fail three times out of four. When tigers hunt buffalo, they fail nine times out of ten. It's tough being a tiger!

Jack Ma Was Rejected by KFC

Jack Ma co-founded *Alibaba* and *AliPay*. In 2017 Jack was listed at Number 2 on Fortune's List of the World's 50 Greatest Leaders. He made a slow start.

Jack came from a poor family in Hangzhou, China.

As a small boy, Jack bought a pocket radio so he could listen to English radio shows every day. From the age of 12 he would ride his bicycle 27 kilometres so he could take tourists around Hangzhou and practise his English. He did this for nine years. Jack failed his middle school exam three times. He failed the entrance exam to Hangzhou Normal University for three consecutive years. After graduating from University, Jack applied for 31 different jobs and received 31 rejections.

He was rejected by the police force! Says Jack, *"I went for a job with KFC. Twenty-four people went for the job. Twenty-three were accepted. I was the only guy rejected!"* Jack bounced back. He became an English teacher.

Then in 1999, he and 17 friends launched Alibaba. It was Jack's third online venture. Alibaba lost money for the first three years, and then became one of the biggest corporations on earth.

Bouncing Back

On failure, Jack says, "Make a lot of mistakes and never give up. I call Alibaba '1,001 MISTAKES!'"

How We Learn

SUCCESS we celebrate – but we don't learn very much.

FAILURE hurts. We contemplate. We ask, *"How can I get fitter, save more, be quicker? How can I learn faster, get help, do better?"*

That's how we get educated.

Persistence Is Not Desperation

Desperate people say, *"If I don't GET this, WIN that, MARRY him, I will die."* That's not helpful.

Achievers are DETACHED.

Detachment is not disinterest.

Detached people say, *"I don't mind how many hours I practise. I don't care how many auditions I do. I don't care how many interviews I attend. I will do this, I will learn this, I will figure this out because it's what I want to do."*

Determination and Detachment

It is possible to be detached and still be very determined. People who are detached and determined know that effort and excellence are ultimately rewarded.

Let's say you apply for a job at *Altitude Airlines*. You are excited about the new job, and you prepare carefully. You tweak your resume. You write out your interview speech and you practise it in front of the bathroom mirror.

You do your online interview, and you give it your best shot.

What next? You get on with your life. You enrol in extra study. You plan your next job application.

If you get hired by *Altitude*, you're happy. If not, you are still moving forward.

Disinterested people say: *"Who cares?"* and *"Why bother?"*

Desperate people say: *"If I don't get this I'll die!"*

When you are determined and detached, you say, *"One way or another, I will get a good job – and I don't care how long it takes."* You tell yourself, *"If I don't win this time, I will win next time or the time after that."*

What Other People Think

Perhaps your dream is to open a restaurant, write a best-selling novel, become an online influencer or study medicine.

If you are like most people, your biggest fear might be, *"What will people think?"* and *"What will people say if I fail?"*

Worrying about what people think is a waste of time. Here's why.

Other people will fall into roughly three groups.

1. People who HOPE YOU'LL SUCCEED. No need to worry about them.
2. People who will be HAPPY IF YOU FAIL. If they can find a way to feel better about themselves, wonderful. No need to worry about them.
3. People who have NEVER HEARD OF YOU – probably about eight billion people. Why worry about them?

Whether you succeed or fail, people care more about their own problems. They may give you a passing thought, but what really matters to them is THEIR mortgage, THEIR back pain and THEIR trip to Disneyland.

Even when we die, everyone gets on with their lives. People move on, whether you are Elvis or the Pope.

Isn't that how it should be?

Bouncing Back

Chase your dream. What other people think of you is none of your business.

> Ever Tried, Ever Failed, No Matter.
> Try Again, Fail Again, Fail Better!
>
> Samuel Beckett

My First Book

The first book I wrote was a children's book. I had heard it can be tough to find a publisher. So I had a plan.

I made a list of the world's 60 major publishers. Then I printed 60 copies of my manuscript and posted a copy to each one.

It seemed a clever strategy. Out of 60 publishers I thought five would like it – or at least three!

After two weeks I got my first "*No*". I kept track of the rejections. Soon I had ten. I ticked them off my list. Then 20, 35, 49, 52, and finally 60 rejections.

Then 61! One publisher sent me the SAME rejection letter TWICE! That hurt!

I was broken-hearted for a week. But I didn't quit. I needed another book.

I spent 18 months writing and illustrating a new manuscript, *Being Happy!* I sent it to 16 publishers – for 16 rejections.

But publisher number 17 said, "*Yes.*" *Being Happy!* has now sold over three million copies.

It took me 77 rejections to get a book published. You might only need 20 or 30 rejections to get your book published. Or you might need a hundred.

Does it matter?

The Big American Launch

Every project has setbacks.

To launch *Being Happy!* in America, we organised a cocktail party for the media at the Australian Embassy on Fifth Avenue in Manhattan.

I was a nobody-author. We wanted to make a flying start. So we sent hundreds of invitations to what seemed like every newspaper, news bureau, TV station, radio station and journalist on the East Coast of the USA.

I flew to New York for the launch.

We knew that not everybody would come. So we catered for two hundred. We had 14 cases of Australian wine – and trays of cheese, crackers, canapes, sandwiches. How many people came to our big launch? Nobody! Zero people.

NOBODY CAME.

That hurt.

If you have ever had a party all by yourself, just you and 11 waiters, you'll know that the service is sensational.

Who Needs Disasters?

"*A team, like men, must be brought to its knees before it can rise again.*"
                                                                    Vince Lombardi

Sometimes we need a smack in the face.

Did you ever do this rollercoaster?

Part 1: **Humility:** You were open to ideas and grateful for any help.
Part 2: **Success:** You were flying high. You knew it all.
Part 3: **Disaster:** You discovered you didn't know it all.
Part 4: **Humility:** You were open to ideas and grateful for any help.

Humility makes us better people: better partners, better parents, better teachers, better students, better friends. With our ego out of the way, we see everything more clearly.

People like to help us when we are humble.

In a Nutshell

Sometimes it takes a disaster to make us humble. Most disasters are not TOTAL disasters.

Asking for Help

What can you do when you are desperate and don't know what to do? You may like to try this. Humbly, sincerely, speak to whatever higher power you believe is behind this exquisite universe, and say, "*I have no answers. Please show me what to do today*".

You probably won't hear a voice from the sky or find a sack of cash on your coffee table. But something will likely happen to help you through the next 24 hours.

You may get a call from a friend, you may stumble on a book or a podcast or an unexpected opportunity – or you might find a little love, encouragement or inspiration out of nowhere, enough to get you through the day.

After you survive your crisis you may look back and wonder, "*Was my call for help really answered? Or would it have happened anyway?*"

How could you ever know? Ask more often.

Despite what we were told by people wanting to put the fear of God into us, the power behind this universe doesn't keep count and doesn't hold grudges.

Whatever challenge you face right now may be here to remind you that you don't have to do it all by yourself.

All of us can receive help and inspiration. We just need to ask. Being angry doesn't help. Being cocky doesn't help.

Bouncing Back

What helps is being humble.

**YOU ARE NEVER BEATEN
UNTIL YOU QUIT**

6

SET A TARGET

It's not failure that crushes us.
What hurts most is never having tried.

**Your plans for tomorrow affect how you live today.
Conquering fear.**

Alex Gonzalex

Alex Gonzalex called me from Mexico to tell me his story.

He began, "At twenty, I had a kind of arthritis. I couldn't get out of bed. A therapist suggested I could help myself by drinking alkaline water for 40 days. No food, just water!"

Alex explained, "I could hardly move. I was in agony. I had nothing to lose. So I tried it."

He said, "After 11 days all my pain disappeared."
I said, "You must have been very happy!"
He said, "I was very hungry!

"But I continued to drink only water for two more weeks. After 25 days, I was so full of energy, I jumped out of bed and ran six miles."

I stopped him.

"Alex, did you eat something before you ran six miles?"
He said, "No! I just ran!"

(I am sharing Alex's story. I am not recommending his diet.)

Already I was amazed. Then he said, "Then I rode a bicycle around the world!"

He explained, "*It took me two years to prepare for the journey and another two years to ride around the world. I wore out four sets of brakes, six bicycle seats, 18 bike chains and 22 sets of tyres.*

"*I got lost in the Gobi Desert for six days with no road, no map and no food. I got arrested in China, and I met Michael Jordan, President Bill Clinton, the King of Spain, Paolo Coelho and the Pope!*"

Spreading Happiness

I said, "*That's incredible. But Alex, why did you call me?*"

He explained, "*I read your book, Being Happy! I realised that I needed a BIG goal and I wanted to spread happiness!*" Alex tells his story in his book, El Mundo en dos Ruedas – The World on two Wheels.

Alex's story is typical of many achievers. ACHIEVERS MOSTLY START FROM WAY BEHIND. A young man who was crippled rode his bike around the planet.

Human beings are amazing. We can BOUNCE BACK. That includes you.

In a Nutshell

If you have less money, less experience and less confidence than you THINK you need, that's probably PERFECT.

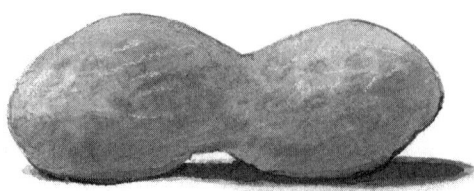

ON CREATING A BETTER LIFE

HERE'S HOW THINGS USUALLY UNFOLD:

FIRST *YOU MAKE THE* **DECISION**.

THEN *COMES THE OPPORTUNITY.*

ANDREW MATTHEWS

Why Set Goals?

Professor Edward Banfield of Harvard University spent much of his career studying why certain people flourish. He found the biggest reason is not our IQ, not education, it's not about having money or who we know.

He found that high achievers have what he called *Time Perspective*. They think about where they want to be in five, ten or even twenty years' time.

We might simply call it planning ahead.

The PLANS YOU HAVE for your career, for your bank balance, for a healthy body, determine what you do today.

Your long-term goals shape the decisions you make today:

- *"Will I read a book or get drunk?"*
- *"Will I save $100 – or blow it?"*
- *"Will I eat an apple – or a pizza?"*

If your goal is to be debt-free or to one day hike in the mountains with your grandchildren, that influences how you live today.

Banfield found that the further we plan ahead, the better. Twenty years is better than five years, and one year is better than a week.

Having *Time Perspective* encourages us to set goals – and setting goals gives us *Time Perspective*.

It doesn't matter which comes first.

Bouncing Back

Your long-term goals are your foundation for a better life.

One Thing Leads to Another

When a bee leaves home each morning, her mission is to make honey to feed her family. She is not thinking about cross-pollinating fruits and flowers or the survival of the plants and animals.

But in collecting pollen, bees help plants to reproduce.

The great teacher, Buckminster Fuller, explained that bees are an example of what he called the *Law of Precession:*

Because a BEE has a goal, unexpected good things happen. When YOU have a goal, unexpected good things happen.

EXAMPLE: You decide to get fit. While jogging around your neighbourhood you discover the perfect apartment to rent. You weren't even looking for a new home. You were jogging.

EXAMPLE: You take a class in photography. You discover that you don't really like taking photos, but you love the teacher. You marry the teacher.

Some of the best things that ever happen to you, happen because you started doing something else.

When I was in my twenties, I began giving weekend seminars – not very successfully. I thought, "*If I write a book, maybe people will take me seriously.*"

I wasn't interested in being a full-time author. I was trying to save my seminar business.

One book led to 12. Books became the main event.

*So often, **new friendships** happen – and **exciting opportunities** appear – when we **least** expect them.*

It's life's way of saying,
"NEVER UNDERESTIMATE THE PRESENT MOMENT."

The Bonus of Setting Goals

Let's say you love making music. You and your friends start a little rock band. Your goal is to make music, but here's what happens:

- You need equipment. So you learn to save money.
- You learn about electronics and audio equipment.
- You study online marketing.
- You learn how to collect money from people who forgot to pay you.

It was originally about music, but look where it took you.

Joanne Learned Japanese

Joanne wanted to learn a language. She chose Japanese.

She became fascinated by everything Japanese. She took vacations in Japan. She got a job with a Japanese company and spent a year in Yokohama, met and married a charming guy called Richiro and now has three children, a Japanese travel agency and a poodle called Yuki.

Her plan was just to learn a language.

Goals take us places we never imagined.

Life Is Like Fishing

Most opportunities, friendships, even romances, happen when you least expect them. It's like going fishing.

YOU LOAD YOUR BOAT WITH GEAR AND LUNCH AND YOU FIND THE PERFECT SPOT...

YOU BAIT YOUR ROD AND WAIT AND WAIT. NOTHING!

YOU CHANGE THE BAIT. YOU SHIFT THE BOAT. NOTHING!

ALL YOU CATCH IS AN OLD BOOT.

AS YOU HEAD FOR HOME, ALONG COMES A BIG SHARK THAT SCARES THE PANTS OFF A BEAUTIFUL LITTLE FISH THAT JUMPS INTO YOUR BOAT!

NO WAY DID YOU EXPECT IT. NO WAY COULD YOU PLAN IT.

When You Least Expect It

How often have you put all your energy into a deal, a project, a relationship that went nowhere? But it led to something else.

Some people would say. *"Don't fish. It's too hard. Stay home!"*

NO. NO. NO! You need to be out there. When you are in the game, going places, trying new things, meeting people, life surprises and delights you.

Bouncing Back

Give your best effort, and when you least expect it, that job opportunity, that key customer, your new boyfriend – or a beautiful fish – will jump into your boat.

Lucky People

How do people get lucky? They get lucky by TRYING THINGS THAT LEAD TO OTHER THINGS.

Whenever you set a goal, whether it's to build a website, breed canaries or save a thousand dollars, you meet people, learn things, go places.

Good things happen that you never imagined.

One thing leads to another.

Isn't that a great reason to get off the couch?

It's What You Become

We sometimes see in the news where a mother of three is rowing a little boat across the Atlantic. Or we read about an accountant who is riding a unicycle around Europe.

Our first reaction might be, *"Why not take a plane?"*

The answer of course is that when you take a boat or a bike, YOU ARE TRANSFORMED BY THE JOURNEY.

Not only do you learn about navigation and faraway places; you learn about yourself.

You discover resilience you didn't know you had.

When you set yourself a goal – whether it's to run a marathon or open an online store or learn Spanish – you arrive a different person.

When you set out to DO SOMETHING EXTRAORDINARY, or CREATE SOMETHING EXTRAORDINARY, or RAISE EXTRAORDINARY CHILDREN, YOU BECOME EXTRAORDINARY.

Your best friend or your brother-in-law may not understand this. They ask, *"Why aim so high? Why stretch yourself?"*

Because you are transformed by the journey.

In a Nutshell

It's not about what you GET. It's what you BECOME in the process.

Goals Make You Happier

Did you ever buy a gym membership, enrol yourself to study something or plan a vacation?

Did you ever decide to tidy your desk?

Instantly you felt happier, like *"I'm taking charge of my life."*

Here's what any psychologist will tell you and what you already know. When we feel helpless or stuck, we get depressed.

When we feel in control, we become happier. This is why setting goals makes us happier. We take more control.

Goals give us something to look forward to. So life feels better.

Big goals, little goals.

Do It for Your Children

You owe it to your kids to fail!

Children need to see how life works. Kids need to understand that you can try and fail, and try and fail – and that to try and fail is something to be proud of.

It's Never Too Late

My mother began writing her first book at 67.

She passed away at 68 and never finished it, but she was happier because she made a start.

If you set a goal to build a business or write a book, and you get hit by a truck, are you going to worry?

What Hurts Most?

It's not failure that crushes us.
What hurts most is never having tried.

When you get to 85-years-old, will you care about the things you tried that didn't work?

Here's what will keep you awake.

What you didn't try! The vacation you didn't take. The time you didn't speak up. The girl in the café that you didn't date. The online business that you almost started.

If you put everything into a project, and fail, you can live with that. When you don't put in an effort, that's what eats away at you.

It's the same with a relationship. What hurts is when you know you could have done more.

When you truly understand that what hurts is never having tried, won't you write that novel, save for that special trip or study for that extra degree?

Won't you launch that project, take an extra risk?

Rebecca's Story

"You run with nothing. You literally run out the door sometimes, and you've got five bucks in your pocket and a cell phone that they are going to cut off at any minute."

Rebecca Bender grew up in a loving family in a small town in Oregon. She was a keen athlete and a top student. Rebecca graduated high school a year early and was accepted into Oregon State University.

Then she got trapped in the Las Vegas sex trade. Says Rebecca:

> For nearly six years I was bought and sold among three different traffickers. Two of them tattooed their names on my back – they branded me like a piece of cattle. My face was broken in five places.

I was hospitalised for dehydration and exhaustion, I was jailed seven times, I attempted suicide twice.

Rebecca explains:

When I was 18, I became a single mother. I went to a party and met this amazing guy. He was funny and charming – the kind of guy that everyone in the room wants to be his friend. He told me he was a record producer.

We dated for six months, and he asked me to move in with him. He got to know my hopes, my dreams, my fears. He soon told me that his job was relocating him to Las Vegas. He said, *"But I can't ask you and the baby to Vegas because that isn't where families live."*

I thought, *"Oh, he thinks we're a family!"* I begged him to take us. I never realised he had been *grooming* me to trust him from day one.

Will I Live or Die?

The first night we were in Vegas – we hadn't even unpacked – he said, *"Get dressed up. I want to take you out on the town."* We left my daughter with his brother.

But instead of going to a nightclub, he took me to a dead-end street. He said, *"This building is an escort service. You need to sign up."*

I thought, *"Escort... that sounds like prostitution!"*

That's when he slapped me across the face. He said, *"I spent a lot of money to get you here. I have paid for the apartment. I filled the fridge with food. You are going to go inside and get my money back."*

My first thought was, *"I don't even know the address where we left my baby!"*

I was trapped. I didn't know what he was capable of – or if I would live or die. I just wanted to get to my baby.

I opened the door and there was a young man. He gave me about $300...

The Gradual Slide

People ask, *"How could you?"*

When you have a trafficker that's waiting at home with your child and he says, *"If you don't bring home $1500 you are going to find your daughter out on the street..."*

It's a gradual slide and suddenly you cross this boundary that you thought you would never cross. I was beaten, brainwashed and drugged. I felt embarrassed, ashamed, unwanted and alone. I was an addict by 21.

People ask, *"Why didn't you try to escape?"*

I tried many times.

You think, *"When I have enough money, when I can get help, when nobody is watching me, when I can safely take my baby..."*

One time I got to the airport only to discover that, after September 11, you can't buy a ticket at an airport with cash.

Running Was Not the Hard Part

Thankfully, in 2006 the federal investigators raided the place where I was living, and my daughter and I were able to escape.

The hard part was starting over at 26, with an eight-year-old girl, being homeless. The hard part was having a criminal record, a huge gap in job history, and more trauma than any person should live with.

The hard part was, *"What now?"*

Rebecca Bounces Back

Says Rebecca:

> I wanted to help stop human trafficking and help survivors. I tried so many things that I thought, "I SHOULD KNOW how to do this," but it didn't go very well! I tried crisis response, and it didn't go well. I tried being an emergency foster parent to a trafficked teen and it didn't go well.

It is okay to try and fail. That's how you learn what you are good at.

How did Rebecca bounce back? The girl who never went to college, the former addict with a criminal record, what did she do?

Rebecca created the *Rebecca Bender Initiative*. She has now trained over 100,000 first responders and professionals to counter human trafficking: FBI agents, undercover cops, homeland security, chiefs of police, childcare professionals, social workers – anybody who can intercept. See www.rebeccabender.org.

Rebecca created the *Elevate Academy*, a school to help survivors of human trafficking. *Elevate Academy* has so far helped about 1,000 students in 12 countries.

Rebecca advises government. She is a member of the *National Advisory Committee on Sex Trafficking of Children and Youth* in the United States.

Rebecca earned her Master's degree. She has four daughters.

On finding your purpose, Rebecca says, *"Just frickin' try it. You don't want to live the rest of your life wondering, 'What if I had gone after my dreams?'"* [11] [12] [13]

Jason's Story

Does it help to have a goal?

- At age three, Jason was diagnosed as severely autistic.
- Jason didn't speak until he was 11.
- He couldn't read or write until he was 18.
- When he was 30, experts told Jason that he *"would need to be housed in assisted living and would need lifelong support as an adult"*.

At 30, Jason was working in a Sainsbury's supermarket.

But Jason surprised the experts. He got two Master's degrees, a post-graduate certificate and a PhD from Liverpool's John Moores University. He then pursued his dream of teaching at a university. He wrote countless academic papers. Says Jason, *"Everything I submitted got violently rejected… I treated it as a learning experience."* Jason never quit.

In 2018, Jason was appointed professor at the University of Glasgow's School of Education. Two more teaching appointments followed. Then in March 2023, Jason Arday was appointed Professor of Sociology at the University of Cambridge – and became Cambridge's youngest black professor.

What got Jason out of a supermarket and into the Number 2 ranked university in the world, in only eight years?

HIs mother never lost faith in him. His college tutor, Sandro Sandi, continually encouraged him. Jason worked hard.

Jason also had a goal. Some time after he learned to write at the age of 18, Jason wrote this on his mother's bedroom wall:

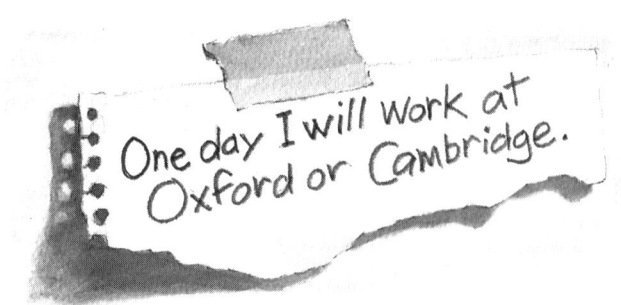

Teuku

I was in a Malaysian shopping mall in 2013 when a man approached me.

He said, *"Are you Andrew Matthews?"*

I sensed he had a story to share. So I invited him to a nearby Starbucks.

He said, *"I'm Teuku from Aceh in Indonesia. My family was very poor.*

"When I was in university, I was so poor that I owned just one pair of trousers. I didn't even own a shirt. My girlfriend would lend me her shirts to wear to school. Many days I had nothing to eat.

"When I was at my lowest point, a friend loaned me the Indonesian version of your book, Being Happy!"

He explained, *"Apart from textbooks, it is the first book I ever read. I realised two things:*

1. *that I could CHOOSE my thoughts*
2. *that I should SET MYSELF GOALS."*

The List

Teuku said, *"I began to have a VISION of the life I wanted. I made a list on a card of everything I wanted for my future:*

- *a degree*
- *a good job*
- *international travel*
- *a family with two children*
- *an apartment*
- *a nice car.*

"I stuck that list on my wall."

He leaned forward, *"Today I am the Asian business development manager for a multi-national corporation."*

He said, *"I travel the world. I have a wife and two beautiful girls who go to international schools."*

He said, *"I still have bad days. So I keep that card – the one with the goals – to remind me how far I have come."*

Dubai

We kept in touch. Teuku was promoted to Global Manager, based in Dubai.

In 2016 I called him.

"Teuku, Julie and I are coming to Dubai on 16 November. Can you join us for dinner at our hotel?"

Teuku said, *"I'm flying to Boston and New York on the 16th. Can you come a day earlier?"* Teuku, THE GUY WHO DIDN'T EVEN OWN A SHIRT, now jets around the globe.

In life you either **MAKE EXCUSES** *or you* **MAKE THINGS HAPPEN.**

Teuku

Julie and I joined Teuku and his beautiful wife, Zizi, for dinner on the 15th. It was Zizi who loaned Teuku her shirts!

Teuku has since been headhunted by another multi-national corporation. I meet up with Teuku almost every year.

What is Teuku proudest of? Not his own achievements. Teuku gets most excited when he talks about his wife and children.

You say, *"Sure, people bounce back – but what if you are BROKE?"*

Bouncing Back

Teuku would tell you to **TAKE CONTROL OF YOUR THOUGHTS, SET SOME GOALS, DO YOUR BEST EACH DAY,** *and extraordinary things will happen.*

Your Long-term Goal

It takes as much energy to wish as it does to plan.

Eleanor Roosevelt

How do you choose a long-term goal? It SHOULD be something that excites YOU. It SHOULD NOT be something you choose to impress people or please your parents.

How long-term is a long-term goal? Maybe six months or a year – or a lifetime.

Are you still looking for a challenge to get you excited? The list below may be a starting point. Don't be limited by this list.

- Create a garden
- Save $5000
- Master a software program
- Learn a new sport
- Learn a musical instrument
- Get fit
- Get a degree
- Take a round-the-world trip with your family
- Learn to cook like a chef
- Write a book
- Eliminate your credit card debt
- Read one book per week for a year
- Build an online business
- Learn public speaking
- Complete a triathlon
- Learn to meditate
- Learn a language
- Learn to dance
- Map your family tree.

Here are some short-term goals you may like to add:
- Be a better friend
- Keep a journal
- Hold a reunion
- Get a medical check-up
- Reconnect with ten old friends
- Declutter your home and office
- Create a household budget
- Join a gym or a sports team.

SEEING THE WHOLE ROAD

You say, "What if I don't know exactly where I am going or how I am going to get there?"

You don't always need to see the whole road.

YOU DON'T ALWAYS HAVE TO **SEE** YOUR DESTINATION.

YOU DON'T NEED TO KNOW **EXACTLY** HOW YOU WILL GET THERE.

JUST TAKE **ONE STEP EACH DAY** AND BELIEVE THAT THINGS WILL WORK OUT.

THAT'S OFTEN ENOUGH.

Imagine you are driving to your friends' house. They live fifty miles from anywhere. It's getting dark and you switch on your headlights. How far can you see? Not 50 miles. Maybe 50 metres.

Do you give up?

No. You keep driving. You drive that first fifty metres and then you can see another 50 metres. You handle what is in front of you. That's enough.

Go as Far as You Can

You conquer fear by facing it. You ask yourself: *"What's the worst that could happen?"* and *"Would I survive?"*

Do you want to be a chef, pilot, artist, entrepreneur, personal trainer? Do all you can. Learn all you can. Go as far as you can.

In six months you will be able to see further.

You can begin building a business without knowing where your customers will come from. You can plan a vacation without knowing where you will stay. You can begin writing a book without knowing who will publish it.

Margot Robbie

"Behind mountains are more mountains."

Haitian proverb

Hollywood actor Margot Robbie reveals how she got her start in TV:

> I was banging down doors. I called Fremantle Media, like, every day until someone made a mistake and put me through to the casting agent for '*Neighbours*'.
>
> That's how I got my audition. I spoke to Jan Russ.
>
> I said, "*I'm in town working on something.*"
>
> She said, "*How old are you?*"
>
> "*I'm seventeen.*"
>
> "*Well, we need a seventeen-year-old girl right now. Come in next week.*"

Says Margot, "*Cold call! Write letters, whatever you gotta do! I STILL DO IT. I still write to people I want to work with.*"

On success, Margot says, "*I thought it would be a mountain, where you get to the top, and then it's like: 'Wheeee! It's so easy after this!'*

"*Any time I get near the top, there's another mountain!*" [14]

Why Not Me?

I grew up believing that certain special people were "chosen" to live exciting lives – or to be high achievers – and then, there was the rest of us.

Well, I have been speaking at conferences for 33 years. At these conferences there are other speakers – sporting greats, famous authors, movie stars, professors, prime ministers, billionaires. I get to meet some of them.

You know what is different about these people? Not much.

They are average people – except at some point they got serious.

They said:

"WHY NOT ME?"
"WHY NOT NOW?"

God is never going to come down from a cloud and say, *"You now have permission to be successful!"*

Bouncing Back

It's not that some higher power decides, "You get to be a movie star" or "You have to dig ditches!"

You choose it. It is a decision that comes from deep within you: "I AM READY TO DO WHATEVER IT TAKES."

WHAT'S THE DIFFERENCE
BETWEEN A **DREAM** AND A **GOAL**?
A **GOAL** HAS A PLAN.

WE BECOME WHAT WE THINK ABOUT.

YOU DON'T ACHIEVE GREAT THINGS BY **LOOKING *AT WHO YOU ARE.***

YOU ACHIEVE GREAT THINGS BY FOCUSING ON *WHO YOU WANT TO BE.*

7

IMAGINE A BETTER LIFE

For life to get better we must see it as better.
We become what we think about.

Why willpower is never enough.
The power of your imagination.

Alfred's Story

"Growing up, I dreamed of being an artist and sailing ocean yachts."

Alfred Engel grew up in poverty in post-war Austria. Says Alfred:

> My teachers warned me that if I failed at everything, I would end up a street sweeper.
>
> My father was a street sweeper. So I was ashamed of my father. I was ashamed because he was ashamed. My father drank to hide his shame. He wasn't the angry alcoholic, more the quiet underachiever.
>
> As a kid I was surrounded by failure – mostly my own. Each year at school, I got the worst possible marks without having to repeat a grade. That was my greatest achievement.
>
> **My Banking Career**
>
> I lived in fear. When I was 15 a teacher got me a job in a bank licking stamps. I was nervous amongst men in suits. When I saw people in the corridor, I hid behind a cupboard. The bank would send me on ten-minute errands to the post office next door. I would take five hours. I wasn't misbehaving. I was too terrified of my colleagues to return to work.

After five months of waiting five hours for me to find my way back from the post office, they sacked me.

My closest friends either died early or went to jail.

At 17 I got a job as an apprentice signwriter. I loved painting signs. Next to being an artist, which was my crazy fantasy, it seemed like the perfect job. I was the top apprentice in Austria three years running. This could have been the beginning of a better life, but instead it nearly killed me.

I desperately wanted to be somebody. I wanted to be a businessman. So I started a signwriting business. I had my own recipe for success: *if you have no work, employ more people!* Soon I had four employees and no work. I was so stupid!

My Green Period

I starved. For weeks I wouldn't have a penny to buy even a potato. I remember searching my apartment, desperate for anything to eat. I would find half-eaten slices of bread in the back of a cupboard, cut off the green bits and soak them in water to make them chewable. I ate mouldy crusts that I found under the rug.

I was sick with stress. Every morning I coughed up a strange green slime. That was my green period.

Somehow my business lasted five years. I was terrified, traumatised and eventually, hospitalised. I had a total nervous breakdown. I spent two months in hospital, and by the time I was released, I had been declared bankrupt.

Having done very little for five years, I did absolutely nothing for the next two. I felt useless, and I was broke. It seemed like a good time to leave the country.

I heard that Australia was looking for signwriters and I decided to migrate. *Australia needed me!*

A New Start

I made two critical decisions when I left Europe. I decided I would:

- never again spend money I don't have
- never again pretend to be someone I'm not.

Sometimes you meet someone who changes your destiny. In Australia, when I was 32, I met Peter Matthews. He became both my best friend and my mentor.

Peter was a successful landscape artist. For the first time, I saw that it was possible to make a living doing what I had only dreamed about. Peter showed faith in me and taught me how to be a better artist and a better person.

I painted every day and studied art books every night. Within a year or so I was selling my own work. Soon I began teaching watercolour painting. I was fortunate to win some big art competitions, and I was on my way.

Alfred Engel became one of Australia's most successful artists, winning dozens of awards and selling his works for tens of thousands of dollars. He built and sailed two beautiful ocean-going yachts and was elected deputy mayor of my hometown, Victor Harbor.

My Dad was Alfred's mentor. Alfred is one of mine. What did I learn from Alfred?

- **When you have a dream,** find someone who is living your dream. Even if you can't meet them, learn everything about them. Learn how they think, how they work, how they plan, how they breathe!
- **A better life begins with a VISION for a better life.**

Arnie's Story

"If my life was a movie, no one would believe it."

Arnie also grew up in Austria. At 15, Arnie saw the movie, *Hercules*, starring bodybuilder, Reg Park. Arnie began to imagine himself as a champion bodybuilder, a movie star, a businessman – and an American!

Arnie began working out.

Arnold Schwarzenegger won 7 *Mr Olympia* bodybuilding titles and 4 *Mr Universe* titles.

Then movies. Arnie's first movie, *Hercules in New York*, was a flop. Says Arnie, "I was told by agents and casting people that my body was 'too weird', that I had a funny accent, and that my name was too long. You name it, and they told me I had to change it… EVERYWHERE I TURNED, I WAS TOLD THAT I HAD NO CHANCE."

Arnie didn't make another movie for five years.

"I'll be back!"

Arnie never quit.

Despite his thick Austrian accent, Arnold Schwarzenegger, became one of Hollywood's biggest action heroes. He made over 40 movies including *The Terminator* and *Total Recall*.

He earned a business degree. He became an American.

In 2003, Arnold Schwarzenegger was elected governor of California and named by *Time Magazine* as one of the *100 Most Influential People in the World*.

How important is your mental picture?

Says Arnie, "I saw myself on that Mr Universe stage. I saw my career in front of me. And it's not a dream.

"YOU HAVE TO HAVE THE VISION and then if you follow that, miracles can happen."

Jimmy's Story

In 2017 Jimmy Kalb's company, *Triad Components Group*, was named by *Forbes Magazine* as one of the 25 Best Small Businesses in the USA. It didn't come easily.

Jimmy recalls:

> I grew up outside San Francisco. I was the oldest of five kids. My parents were habitual drug users. Mum smoked marijuana daily. Dad did cocaine and other hard drugs. My dad also ran an illegal betting operation.
>
> My parents took little interest in our lives or our education. We lived on food stamps. We wore second-hand clothes.
>
> I lived in constant fear that the police would raid our home and either arrest my parents or put us kids in foster care.
>
> **Failing at San Diego State**
>
> I was accepted into San Diego State University. I studied electrical engineering – and consistently failed. I would get Ds, Fs and occasionally a C minus.
>
> I worked to put myself through college: in factories, in retail, in construction, in restaurants, as a bus boy, at PBS TV. It was hard.
>
> If you failed a subject at San Diego State, you could retake the exam during summer vacation. That's the only reason I graduated.
>
> I knew I would never be a great engineer. So I got a job as a technical sales representative. My territory was Eastern Europe, the Middle East and Africa.
>
> Suddenly, I was travelling the world and staying in Hilton Hotels. Meanwhile, my buddies were backpacking. It felt pretty good.
>
> After my six years as a sales representative, a buddy and I started a part-time business called Vortex Technologies. We imported electrical components from Asia and sold them to factories in the USA and Mexico. I kept my regular job.

Flying High

Vortex did well. We turned over $65,000 the first year, a quarter of a million the second year. I quit my day job to work at Vortex full-time. I married my college sweetheart, and we had two children.

Soon, Vortex had 15 staff. Success seemed easy. I was blowing money, flying business class. I thought I knew it all.

The Death Spiral

By 2000, American factories were relocating to China, and all our customers began to disappear!

In 2001 my wife and I separated. I now had two households to support.

By 2002, our sales were in free-fall. I thought, *"This will turn around."* I borrowed more and more money to pay wages and rent.

I told myself, *"Next year will be better!"* But we were in a death spiral that lasted EIGHT YEARS. Then came the Global Financial Crisis!

By August 2009, we were down to four staff. I called a final meeting. I said, *"Guys, we have enough cash left for two weeks and then we need to close. Thank you for everything. You have been great."*

Hours later, my staff came to me and said, *"If we take a 30% pay cut, and if the landlord will halve the rent, we can last a bit longer."*

Our Compass

We were desperate. The five of us sat down and asked ourselves, *"What do we stand for? What do we want to achieve as a company?"*

We agreed on four core values:

1. **Highest Integrity.** Always tell our customers the truth.
2. **Transparency.** Constant communication within our company and with our customers.
3. **Education.** Never stop learning!
4. **Have Fun.**

These values became our compass. One of our team was an artist. So she painted a giant compass – and our values – on the office wall. WE NOW HAD A SHARED VISION.

We survived August. We made some sales in September. We found some new customers. The landlord halved the rent. Things got better and better.

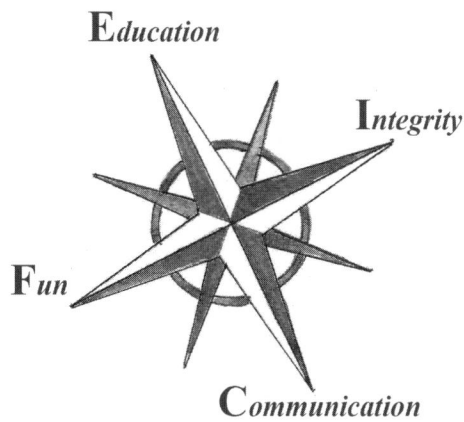

Our company has a mission. We employ people who may not get a chance elsewhere. For example:

- Carol was our website builder for 20 years. Carol has cerebral palsy. She inspired us all.

- Duane is our customer service guy. When Duane came to us, he was wearing an ankle bracelet – he was on work release from prison. We gave him a chance. He gave us everything he had. Our company would not have survived without Duane.

- Raniah, our graphic artist, is a refugee. She and her family escaped ISIS in Iraq. When she came to us, she spoke only broken English.

For the last twelve years we have averaged 20% growth. But the *Forbes Small Business Award* is not just about growth. It's given to companies that live their values. That makes us all proud.

You say, *"But Jimmy's story is about business. What does Jimmy's story have to do with me?"*

Jimmy's story is about having a VISION. Success begins with a clear vision – for a company AND for a person: *"This is where I am going. This is who I am becoming."*

HOW DO I CHANGE?

*The **mental picture** you have of yourself made you who you are today.*

*When you **change that picture** you have of yourself, **you will change** to match the picture.*

Success Starts in Your Imagination

For life to get better, you hold it in your mind. You do the work. Then it happens.

What does every Masters Golf champion say? What does any Oscar winner say? *"I imagined this as a child. I pictured myself here."*

We become what we think about.

Your MENTAL PICTURE is your most POWERFUL TOOL. Every day before you even get out of bed, this is what you do. See yourself as:

- CONFIDENT
- CRUSHING YOUR TARGETS
- HAPPY.

Even happiness starts as an idea. You must see yourself as happy first. You have a picture.

Your dream job, a loving relationship, more money, first happens in your mind. You begin to picture what you want. You don't need to know exactly how it will happen.

YOU BEGIN TO FEEL IT LIKE IT HAS ALREADY HAPPENED. As you get comfortable with your goal, you notice opportunities. You attract people, "coincidences", even money.

What happened in your mind begins to happen in your life.

Is there work? Always!

Is it easy? No. But here's the point…

It all starts in your mind.

Confidence in public speaking happens in your mind first. More money in the bank: you see it in your mind first. A loving relationship: you see it in your mind first.

Your dream job: you picture yourself working in hospitality or travel or IT. You hold it in your mind. You study. You do the work. It happens – but it FIRST happened in your mind.

A BETTER LIFE BEGINS IN YOUR IMAGINATION.

IN YOUR SPARE MOMENTS, SEE YOURSELF AS HAPPY, PROSPEROUS AND LOVED.

Two Buddies Play-acting

In the 1970s Fred Couples and Jim Nantz were buddies at the University of Houston. Fred was a dedicated golfer with dreams of winning the US Masters, and Jim had ambitions of becoming a top sports announcer.

Together, they would often play-act a scene where Fred, having just won the US Masters, was interviewed by the CBS announcer, Jim Nantz.

In 1992, Fred won the Masters. He was ushered into the Butler Cabin to receive the famous green jacket – and there, to get the inside story, was CBS's Jim Nantz.

At the close of the interview they embraced with tears in their eyes, no doubt reflecting on how the imaginary scene that they had so often rehearsed in Houston had just unfolded before the world in Atlanta.

Would Fred Couples have won the Masters Golf Championship without the play-acting? Would Jim Nantz have achieved his dream without the play-acting? Would it all have happened anyway?

In a Nutshell

There's not a successful actor, astronaut, brain surgeon, pilot, president or pop star who didn't imagine their dream over and over and over again long before it happened.

Justin's Story

In the 1990s I met a young cricketer, Justin Langer.

If you have never seen cricket, it's different! An international cricket match can last five days! In baseball, batters might hit one run. In cricket, a batter can hit 20 or 50 runs – even a hundred runs in one innings.

For millions of children growing up in England, Australia, India, Pakistan and a dozen other nations, their ambition is to play cricket for their country.

Justin Langer had played a few games for Australia and was then dropped from the team. He wondered, *"Will I ever play for my country again?"*

We chatted about visualisation and the subconscious mind.

I said to Justin, *"It's not just about how well you hit the ball. You must feel that you BELONG in the Australian team.*

"If you can't SEE YOURSELF as an international cricketer, if you don't FEEL you deserve it, it doesn't matter how brilliant you are. Your subconscious mind will find ways to sabotage your career.

"But if you SEE YOURSELF as an international star, and FEEL you deserve it, the rest will fall into place."

Justin Bounces Back

I lost touch with Justin, but I began to see him on TV. Justin became a star cricketer.

Twenty-five years later, when he was appointed coach of the Australian Cricket Team, I saw Justin interviewed in a podcast. Justin said:

> I met a guy by the name of Andrew Matthews who was a motivational speaker, author... I got to meet him in Adelaide. I got his book.
>
> You know how most authors write, *"Dear Justin, Good Luck."* He drew this cartoon of me in 1993 with my Australian cap on... and up on the scoreboard he wrote, *"Justin Langer 250"*.

> That's 1993 – Andrew spoke to me about visualising, setting goals.
>
> I began to picture myself scoring 250 runs.
>
> You know what my highest score in test cricket was? Ten years later at the Boxing Day test against England... 250!! ON THE DOT! That's freaky. Work that out!

Two hundred and fifty runs is a massive score. In 180 years of international cricket, only a few dozen players have hit 250 runs.

Justin wrote it down.
He pictured it.
He achieved it.

In 2021, Justin coached the Australian team to a world championship.

What does this have to do with you?

Whatever you want to do that seems impossible, you write it down. You picture it. You keep working toward it.

That goal takes hold in your subconscious. Amazing things happen.

This is the secret of champions. Success happens first in your mind. Reality follows.

How We Create Life-changing Habits

Let's say you want to create a new habit. You want to:

- save money every week
- be tidy, or
- get fit.

What will be most helpful? Will it be:

1. Willpower, or
2. Having a clear goal?

WILLPOWER is not enough. If you see yourself as a couch potato, willpower will never keep you at the gym. In a battle between

"COUCH POTATO"

willpower and your self-image, your self-image will always win.

A CLEAR GOAL is not enough. Lots of people have a clear goal – to be skinny or to save for the future – but never do anything about it.

You can have a clear goal – to eat more vegetables and less junk. Most people know what they should eat – but they don't.

What's most important is:

   3. HOW YOU SEE YOURSELF

Everything changes when you say to yourself, "THIS IS WHO I AM".

For example, you begin to see yourself as the kind of person who:

- does ten minutes of daily exercise
- keeps a tidy home
- meditates daily
- gets enough sleep.

In a Nutshell

New habits are LESS about discipline and MORE about who you are becoming.

As you become that person in your mind, the rest will happen.

YESTERDAY
I WAS CLEVER
SO I WANTED
TO CHANGE
THE WORLD!

TODAY
I AM WISE
SO I AM
CHANGING
MYSELF.

Rumi

8

WHAT NOW?

Everything Is Connected

Have you noticed that:

- when you eat better you feel more like exercising
- when you exercise you eat better
- when you are happier at home you are happier at work
- when you are happier at work you are happier at home?

Everything is connected.

Maybe you are feeling stuck or overwhelmed.

You ask, "*Where do I start to build a better life?*"

It doesn't matter so much WHERE you start, but THAT you start SOMEWHERE!

You may choose to get fit or work at a relationship. You may put more love into your work. You may tidy your bedroom.

Suddenly, you feel better. Suddenly, you have more energy for other parts of your life. Now you are on your way!

Bouncing Back

The key is to START somewhere. ANYWHERE!

"WHAT YOU SEEK IS SEEKING YOU."
Rumi

"I Knew It Would Happen"

People in happy relationships sometimes say, *"I knew there was someone out there just for me."*

People who love where they live sometimes say, *"We knew we would find the right place for us."*

It's like they knew, *"It will happen when the time is right."*

What You Seek

Life doesn't have to be a grim struggle. Persistence matters, but it can be a joyous persistence.

Are you looking for a JOB you can love? There is an employer out there who wants you just as much.

Are you looking for a LIFE PARTNER you can love? There is someone out there who wants you just as much.

Sometimes we get desperate, and our desperation somehow pushes things away. A little shift in thinking can help, to something like, *"It's there for me, and when the time is right it will appear. Until then, I'm happy anyway."*

What you seek is seeking you.

Bouncing Back

Are you struggling, hurting, heartbroken? I sincerely hope BOUNCING BACK! will be helpful.

I have shared 63 stories and 94 cartoons amongst these 27,000 words, to make **three points:**

1. **Most disasters are not TOTAL disasters.**
2. **We ALL doubt ourselves. We ALL have setbacks, and everybody hurts.**
3. **Life can be even BETTER after disappointments and disasters.**

Do you sometimes quit too soon?

These are your 7 Steps to Bouncing Back

1. Find Purpose in Whatever Happens
What makes you extraordinary? Facing challenges you didn't choose.

2. Accept What You Can't Change
Acceptance allows you to move on. Acceptance is power.

3. Look for Good Things Every Day
You find in life what you look for.

4. Live One Day at a Time
Refuse to worry about what you can't fix today. Just give your best until bedtime.

5. When You Fall, Get Back Up!
Daily persistence creates surprising results.

6. Set a Target
It's not failure that crushes you. What hurts most is never having tried.

7. Imagine a Better Life
For life to get better you must see it as better. You become what you think about.

Did you ever read a book, and a month later you couldn't remember what it was about?

The full-colour poster at the link below is for you to pin on your wall. It's your reminder.

Print it out, big or small.

Pin it up at work. Share it with your family.

Get it now: www.andrewmatthews.com/poster

Do YOU have a story?

I have begun writing BOUNCING BACK 2.

Do you have a story that can inspire others – about yourself or someone else? Please tell me.

Contact me at www.andrewmatthews.com/contact

References

1 Inchauspé, Jessie. Glucose *Revolution*. Penguin, 2022. p 7-10

2 Oatlands Crash – Leila and Danny Abdallah. 6 May 2021 **https://www.youtube.com/watch?v=Ho-0IDO7O6g**

3 Hunter, Cheryl. Wabi-sabi: The magnificence of imperfection. TEDx Santa Monica, 2013

4 Harris, Russ. *The Reality Slap*. (2020). Exisle Publishing, 2020.

5 Gilbert, Daniel. The surprising science of happiness. TED, 2012. **https://www.youtube.com/watch?v=4q1dgn_C0AU&t=564s**

6 Donnelly-Emery, Joan. *Chicken Soup for the Soul: Tough Times Won't Last but Tough People Will*. Chicken Soup for the Soul, 2021.

7 Edgley, Ross. *The Art of Resilience: Strategies for an Unbreakable Mind and Body*. Harper Collins, 2021.

8 Lopez, Shane. The secrets of people who love their jobs. TEDx Lawrence **https://www.youtube.com/watch?v=F9b0fi7p3Ts**

9 Lopez, Shane. Focusing on your strengths. (2015). TEDx UCCS **https://www.youtube.com/watch?v=tlFPVhfPzNA**

10 PCP-laced chowder derails *Titanic* filming. **https://ew.com/article/1996/09/13/pcp-laced-chowder-derails-titanic-filming/**

11 Rebecca Bender's story – human trafficking survivor. **www.youtube.com/watch?v=jHcoEY6gJJ0**

12 1 Girl Revolution. Rebecca's story: Trafficked into the sex industry: Persevering to freedom and empowering other women. Episode 76. **https://1girlrevolution.com/rebecca-bender/#:~:text=Rebecca%20Bender%20is%20a%20survivor,recognized%20expert%20on%20human%20trafficking**

13 The Rebecca Bender Initiative. **https://rebeccabenderinitiative.org/**

14 Margot Robbie's secret techniques for auditioning success. The Graham Norton Show Series 26, Episode 18, 2023. **https://www.youtube.com/watch?v=raJZsO-pOhc**